Awakened Empath

The Ultimate Guide to Emotional, Psychological, and Spiritual Healing

Eternal, wise &infinitely eairy being of light.

Luna and Sol

Copyright

Awakened Empath: The Ultimate Guide to Emotional, Psychological, and Spiritual Healing

Table of Contents

A PRAYER FOR THE OVERWHELMED

Oh, sweetheart.
Life is overwhelming for you at times, I know.
Don't listen to the ones who call you over-sensitive or too weak
for this world.
Your sensitivity is exquisitely beautiful!
But you must learn to stay close to yourself.
You must learn to breathe.
To invite curious attention deep into your body.

Allow yourself to feel overwhelmed,
and you won't be overwhelmed, I promise.
It's just a feeling.
A precious part of you longing for love.
It will pass when it's ready.
Let it stay awhile.

Don't pretend to be strong, the one who has it all "figured out."
There will be time for answers soon enough.
Now, simply give "the overwhelmed one" safe passage in your
heart.
Drench the feeling of overwhelm with gentle attention; bathe it in
overwhelming love.

It's okay to feel overwhelmed sometimes, it really is.
Even the strongest feel overwhelmed, for their strength lies in
their vulnerability.

Your sensitive nervous system is perfect, and I love you for it.

And it's all okay, here.
It's really okay, here in the arms
of the present moment.

– Jeff Foster

For all the sensitive and empathic souls out there who feel overwhelmed, isolated, depressed or lost in this world. May you discover just how strong, gifted, and sacred you are.

Introduction

Everything feels like a blur.

You look around and you see a crowd of faces. You feel the movement of feet, bodies, and emotions whirling around you. You feel a clash of emotion in your body: excitement, frustration, joviality, annoyance, and angst mixed together. Your breathing starts to become rapid and shallow. You begin to feel anxious, dizzy, and desperate to leave. There is too much going on. There are too many types of energy here. It all feels like too much. These people are exhausting you.

Stop for a moment and take a deep breath. How do you feel when you read this? Can you relate to this experience? If this scenario sounds familiar, you are almost certainly an empath.

Originating as a word once only used in paranormal and science fiction shows such as *Star Trek*, *Charmed*, and *The Ghost Whisperer*, the term "empath" has now come to describe an innate gift carried by certain people in our society.

As opposed to empathy, which is the ability to understand the emotions of others, an empath is a person who can actually *experience* another's emotions as their own. Empaths have the ability to assimilate the emotions and even the physical sensations of others, making them deeply attentive, warm, compassionate, and insightful people. But, on the other hand, such a high degree of sensitivity to other people's emotional energy is also what makes empaths so prone to issues such as anxiety, depression, and stress-related illnesses. When left unmanaged, this gift can result in feeling overwhelmed and chronically drained by others, and even in being emotionally preyed upon.

According to research conducted by psychologist Elaine Aron at Stony Brook University in New York, 20% of the population are genetically predisposed to be more aware and empathic.[1] And while the number of empaths in our population has never been verified or tested before, this small percentage indicates that empaths are something of a minority in our society; even a rarity. Some authors have even speculated that empaths comprise only about 2-4% of society.[2] However, this percentage could be far greater.

So how can you tell whether you're an empath? There are a number of signs you should look out for, such as:

- You've been told that you're "too sensitive" or intense – and people have told you to "get a thicker skin."
- You tend to absorb the emotional energy of others.
- You have a hard time distinguishing your emotions from other's emotions.
- You feel like a tuning fork that picks up on even the subtlest shifts in another person's mood or energy.
- You find it unbearable to watch any form of violence, cruelty or torture because it causes you intense pain and discomfort.
- You feel dizzy, fatigued, anxious or overwhelmed in crowds of people (such as in supermarkets, stadiums, and malls).
- You absorb or feel the physical symptoms of another ailing friend or family member (e.g. aches, pains, cold symptoms, injuries, etc.).
- You struggle with chronic fatigue.

- You are highly intuitive and tend to make decisions based on your "hunches" or gut feelings.
- You have a strong desire to ease the suffering of others.
- You often play the counsellor or confidant role in your relationships.
- You're often treated as an "emotional dumping ground" by others.
- You are a skilled listener.
- You seem to attract wounded and needy people or "energy vampires."
- You feel drawn to supporting and giving a voice to the underdogs of life.
- You feel a deep connection to nature and animals.
- You are highly creative.
- You need regular periods of solitude to recharge your energy.
- You are drawn to the metaphysical or spiritual side of life.
- You don't function well in unpleasant, chaotic, or overly stimulating situations.
- You can feel the energy of inanimate objects such as food, places, and stones.
- You struggle with sacral, solar plexus, and heart chakra issues such as unstable blood pressure, digestive and lower back problems (e.g. IBS, weight issues, and stomach ulcers).

How many of these signs do you resonate with? If you could relate to more than half of these signs, you're most likely an empath.

Who This Book is For

An interesting phenomenon is happening in the world as we speak. Not only are we evolving on a material level as a species, but we are also evolving psychologically and spiritually. The more accelerated our lives become and the more distant from the inner self we end up being, the more separate we feel from our Souls. As a result, more and more empaths and sensitive people are beginning to reach a "breaking point" in which something in their lives absolutely has to change. It is simply becoming too stimulating, stressful, and demanding to live lives disconnected from our inner source of power.

Because of this widespread suffering, we have written this book to help you explore and navigate the waters of your inner self, and most importantly, how to rediscover emotional, psychological, and spiritual freedom as an empath. Even if you don't 100% identify as an empath but you still understand that you're deeply sensitive, this book will be of great use to you.

Both of us also want to educate your loved ones and peers. This book is for any family members, coworkers, bosses, therapists or romantic partners of yours wishing to gain more clarity and insight about you.

Our Stories

So who are we? We are partners, spiritual mentors, and empaths who have united to fulfil our life purpose of helping others. Since birth we both felt the world deeply and intensely in different ways. Although we both came from polar opposite backgrounds, we both experienced difficult and emotionally tense childhoods.

On one side of the spectrum, I was raised in an extremely strict fundamentalist religion with parents who equated the church as family. There was a kind of silent emotional coldness that emanated in my family; a numb emptiness. Being God-fearing people, my parents brought their interpretation of the Bible into every facet of my life. Although I knew they had good intentions, I couldn't help but feel trapped, unseen, judged, and undervalued. All the repressed and shunned emotions that were deemed as "ungodly" weren't hidden from me. I could feel everything my family was repressing: all the anger, judgement, hatred, sadness, and fear. Through the years, these hidden away emotions began to seriously impact my mental, emotional, and physical health. The older I got, and the more I felt, the more depressed, anxious, and withdrawn I became as an empath. I seemed to absorb their fear and self-loathing like a sponge. On top of that, I also felt incapable of dealing with my own emotions as I was taught to not acknowledge or even care about them. I was thought of as the "responsible" child in the family, and I desperately wanted to cling to that approval. But eventually, as the pain became too much, I began to self-harm and lock myself away as a coping mechanism to stop the pain I felt in my family, peers, and inner self. Finally, I managed to escape from that environment in my early twenties, and have never looked back since.

On the other side of the spectrum was Sol and his upbringing. Raised in an extremely libertine and emotionally explosive family, Sol moved around frequently as a child and had lived in three different continents by the age of eight. As the first born son of a bipolar mother and drug addict father, Sol's entrance

5

into this world was chaotic and unstable from the start. The older he grew, the more he struggled to understand and cope with his family's tendency towards chaos and self-destructive behavior. As the eternal "new kid," he rarely stayed in one place long enough to form connections or bonds with others, making life often extremely lonely. On top of his troubling childhood was his uncle, a schizophrenic, who would have violent outbursts and spontaneous suicide attempts, leading to the feeling of constant anxiety and endangerment. While there were brief periods of calm, they never lasted long. There would always be some new source of anxiety, whether it be visits from the police or the hysterical behavior of his mentally ill mother. With all of these intense and conflicting energies overwhelming him all the time, Sol eventually decided to disconnect from the world as a way of not having to deal with anyone, and search for answers within.

It is very difficult to summarize in just a few paragraphs how much pain we have experienced in our lives. For a long time we both felt lost, confused, fearful, unsafe, and endlessly overwhelmed in this world as sensitive people. But the strange thing about pain is that it has a way of making you strong. Pain gives you perspective and raw experience, and it was thanks to our difficult childhoods that we have both developed the wisdom and insight to help others with their pain today.

What You Will Learn in This Book

Our intention for this book is to help you find peace, understanding, acceptance, and love for who you are as an empath. No matter how lost or at odds with life you are, we have written this book as a blueprint that will help you to develop physical, mental, emotional, and spiritual balance as a sensitive being. In other words, you can think of this book as your personal empath bible! It doesn't matter how much of a beginner you are, or how advanced on your path you may be; you will still benefit directly from this book.

Drawing on our own life experience as empaths, spiritual mentors, and authors of some of the most popular empath resources on the internet, we will share with you how to liberate yourself from anxiety, fatigue, unhealthy habits, and energetic burnout.

Some of the many topics we cover in this book include:

- Empaths and the Shadow Self
- What science, psychology, shamanism, and mysticism say about being an empath
- Types of empath gifts
- Empaths, friendships, and relationships
- How to handle narcissists and energy vampires
- How to parent empath children
- Empaths and the spiritual awakening process
- How to set boundaries as an empath
- How to practice self-love as an empath
- How to ground yourself as an empath
- How to explore your mistaken beliefs as an empath
- How to cleanse and purify your energy as an empath
- Your spiritual purpose as an empath
- … and much more

We have poured tons of our love, energy, and intention into this book with the hopes of helping you to reconnect and awaken to your inner source of wisdom and strength. There is so much this book can offer you in terms of insight, inspiration, and guidance. In fact, we have dedicated almost half of this book to sharing practical and detailed soulwork practices that you can implement into your life.

As you progress through these pages, may you be inspired to honor, nurture, and empower yourself as a sensitive and empathic being. You are a pioneer and trailblazer of humanity, a model for others on how to be sensitive and powerful. This sacred opportunity is entirely up to you to explore, embody, and share with this world. May this book help you on your path; you deserve every bit of loving guidance life can offer.

Chapter 1 – What is Your Empathic Gift?

The majority of human beings have the capacity to sense the emotions, thoughts, and physical sensations of others. But as empaths, we not only sense these inner workings but actually absorb and *embody* them entirely.

Derived from the Greek word "em" (in) and "pathos" (feeling), the term "empath" refers to a person who is able to "feel into" the feelings of others. But although our ability to feel into the emotions of others is an extraordinary gift, it can also be bittersweet. On one hand, we feel an immense sense of connection and compassion towards other people and all of life on earth. We are blessed with the ability to feel emotions such as love, awe, passion, and excitement to a profoundly intense and breathtaking degree. Being empathic also means that we're highly intuitive, creative, and often spiritually gifted. But on the other hand, we also soak up all of the dark and disturbing energy around us. We often spend our days feeling physically ill, exhausted, stressed, or emotionally fragile and triggered by the smallest situations. Coming in contact with a person carrying heavy negative energy can leave us feeling sick and drained for days. *This is how I feel all of the time.*

Because we were never taught how to use our empathic gifts, many of us feel as though we are constantly drowning or paralyzed and overwhelmed by daily life. The more people we come in contact with, the more sick, burdened, and anxious we feel. Deep down, many of us empaths wonder "Is there something wrong with me?" In fact, you might have even sought out psychiatric or medical treatment, but found that the diagnosis you were given just doesn't feel right or match what you're truly experiencing. Many empaths are diagnosed with chronic illnesses such as fibromyalgia, CFS, lupus, and various other autoimmune diseases, as well as psychological disorders such as agoraphobia, social anxiety, ADHD, depression, sensory processing disorder, among many others.

As we'll further explore in this book, the sickness and emotional strain that we experience as empaths is both energetic and psychosomatic in origin. This means that most of our suffering comes from taking on the energy of others and not being able to let this energy flow in and out of us. When energy becomes stuck in our bodies, minds, and energy fields, we experience what is known in the psychiatric field as psychosomatic illness – or illness that originates from an accumulation of psychological and emotional stress.

So, are you an overwhelmed empath? Try to answer the following questions with "yes" or "no."

Empath Wellness Self-Assessment

1. Do you feel overwhelmed, anxious, dizzy or sick when you walk into crowded places? *yes*

2. Do you constantly feel responsible for other people's happiness? *yes*

3. When you feel anxious, do you turn to food, shopping, alcohol, drugs, cigarettes, video games, TV, or other addictions to make you feel better? *yup*

4. Do you struggle with chronic physical illnesses such as headaches, migraines, colds, flus, etc.? *not really*

5. Do you feel fatigued for most of the day?

 yes

10

6. Do you experience frequent insomnia? *yes*

7. Do you have a lot of muscle tension in your neck, shoulders, and back? *kind of*

8. Do you experience a rollercoaster of emotions each day which interfere with your ability to be happy and content? *YES*

9. Do you have dissatisfying, toxic, or abusive relationships in your life? *not really*

10. Do you hoard things and surround yourself with clutter (as a way of insulating energy and creating a protective "wall")? *noo?*

11. Do you struggle to distinguish your emotions from others? *YES*

12. Do you frequently feel "taken for granted" or "used" by other people? *yes*

13. Do you feel anxious and/or depressed each day? *YES*

14. Do you feel like the "emotional dumping ground" of other people? *noo*

15. Do you feel like you're going crazy or like there's something fundamentally wrong about you? *YES*

If you answered mostly "yes" to each question, you are a struggling empath who needs support.

If you answered a balanced mixture of "yes" and "no," you are doing okay in some areas but need help in others.

If you answered mostly "no" to each question, you are doing fine.

If you are currently feeling burdened by many of the issues mentioned above, don't worry. Both of us know how depleting and hellish life can become when you feel inundated by tidal waves of energy each day. It's like drowning or suffocating while you're still breathing. With compassion and empathy, we will gently guide you through countless ways to rediscover the balance you have lost through this book. So take a deep breath, and know that you are being held and supported. The exercises and techniques you'll discover in this book will help you find freedom from any emotional burden.

What Type of Empath Are You?

Every empath is unique. While all empaths, to differing degrees, share the ability to soak up the emotions of others, every empath has a different area of energetic "expertise." In other words, we each carry a unique capacity to gather emotional, psychological, and physical information from *different sources* surrounding us that are often inaccessible to the average unreceptive mind. These different areas of energy expertise can be divided into about ten different types of receptivity, which you will read about below.

Pay attention to which of the following empath types you resonate with the most. Keep in mind that while there are ten distinct types of empaths, it is also common to overlap and share a number of different types:

Claircognizant Empaths

Claircognizance means "clear knowing." If you are a claircognizant empath, you will intuit things about other people through feelings that are then translated as thoughts.

Claircognizant empaths tend to possess a strong inner knowing about other people and will immediately "know" when something is off or when someone is lying or hiding something.

Emotional Empaths

To differing degrees, the majority of empaths are emotionally receptive to other people. This means that whatever another person is feeling will be absorbed and internalized. While this gift can be painful and burdensome (for untrained empaths), it helps us to deeply understand other people and develop high levels of compassion, empathy, and wisdom.

Physical Empaths

The second most common type of empath is the physical empath. Such empaths absorb or mirror the illnesses and bodily pains of other people. Physical empaths make highly skilled energy workers, acupuncturists, massage therapists, medical intuitives, and yoga instructors.

Fauna Empaths

Fauna empaths can feel and interact with animals on an energetic level. For example, fauna empaths will know what it's like to be a certain animal, and will deeply understand the animal's needs and struggles. Often, fauna empaths can feel the emotions of other living creatures and suffer greatly when their habitats are destroyed. Historically, there are many examples of fauna empaths who could communicate with animals, such as Saint Francis of Assisi. In mythology, fauna empaths are also symbolized by "shape-shifting" humans.

Flora Empaths

Flora empaths can communicate with trees, flowers, herbs, shrubs, and many other forms of nature, and are able to receive and interpret their highly varied and complex energetic signals. The flora empath will feel most at home in nature and will be able to strongly sense the differing vibrations of plants all around her.

Geomantic Empaths

Geomantic empaths can read the energy and signals transmitted by the earth. Many geomancers experience headaches, pain or anxiety before earthquakes or other natural disasters. It is also common for geomantic empaths to feel ley lines, or the energetic grid that spans across the planet.

Astral Empaths

Astral empaths can either see, hear, feel (or a combination of these senses) and directly experience one or more types of astral beings, be they spirits, angels or interdimensional beings. Thanks to their ability to travel through the various layers of reality, astral empaths often bring back information and knowledge from worlds outside of our physical realm. In a sense, astral empaths possess strong innate shamanic gifts.

Psychometric Empaths

Psychometric empaths have the ability to receive information, energy, and impressions from physical objects such as photographs, clothing, jewelry, books, and so forth. The energy transmitted by these objects is experienced by the psychometric empath as emotions (this ability is also known as "clairtangency"). Just by touching an object, psychometric empaths can receive emotional information about the previous owners. If you feel uncomfortable energy when you use recycled clothing, utensils or furniture, it's likely because you are a psychometric empath.

Precognitive Empaths

Precognitive empaths feel the occurrence of events before they happen. This precognition is usually manifested through dreams, moments of déjà vu, visions or through physical/emotional sensations. For instance, precognitive empaths will often feel a sense of inexplicable dread, anxiety or excitement before a significant event happens such as a birth, death, life change or societal distress (i.e. war).

Telepathic Empaths

Telepathic empaths are able to accurately feel a person's unexpressed thoughts or move onto another's energetic wavelength. A simple example of everyday telepathy can be seen in the moments that we know what someone is going to say before they say it. Telepathy is also often shared between twins and mother-baby connections. Scientists have even carried out scientifically valid experiments that appear to confirm the existence of telepathy.[1] For telepathic empaths, this means receiving information about others in the form of mental pictures, thoughts, or words which then translate into feelings.

Self-Assessment

If you're unsure about what type of empath you are, you might like to take the quick three question quiz below. This short questionnaire isn't meant to definitively "type" you, but offer a potential answer. You can find the extended version of this short test on our website.

Also, remember that it's possible to overlap and share a variety of these empathic gifts. The questions below are simply designed to help you to discover your most dominant gift.

To begin, please select one answer from each question that is most applicable to you:

1. What are you interested in the most?

    a) Growing plants and herbs, and nurturing nature.
    b) Exploring the unseen spirit world.
    c) Collecting beautiful or meaningful objects.
    d) Taking care of animals.
    e) Healing people.
    f) Understanding Mother Earth.
    g) Counseling people.
    h) Exploring my dreams and the unconscious mind.
    i) Exploring tarot, the I Ching, astrology, numerology, etc.
    j) Understanding the psychology of other beings.

2. What word are you drawn to the most?

    a) Nature
    b) Ethereal
    c) Ancient
    d) Wild

e) Sensual
f) Landscape
g) Compassion
h) Subconscious
i) Wisdom
j) Perception

3. Which statement do you most frequently experience?

a) You can tap into the energetic frequencies of trees, flowers, and plants.
b) You can interact with spirits.
c) You can touch a physical object and immediately receive a story about it.
d) You can understand and interact with animals on a very deep level.
e) When you're around a physically ill person, you can feel their illness in your body.
f) You can always sense the specific "vibe" of a building, landscape or place.
g) You can sense the hidden emotions of other people.
h) You have dreams that predict future events.
i) You always seem to intuitively know what is true and false.
j) You can accurately read the unexpressed thoughts of others.

What's your tally? If you answered mostly:

a) You're a *Flora Empath.*
b) You're an *Astral Empath.*
c) You're a *Psychometric Empath.*
d) You're a *Fauna Empath.*
e) You're a *Physical Empath.*

17

f) You're a *Geomantic Empath.*
g) You're an *Emotional Empath.*
h) You're a *Precognitive Empath.*
i) You're a *Claircognizant Empath.*
j) You're a *Telepathic Empath.*

If you answered different letters to each question you likely have more than one predominant empathic gift.

Once you've found out your result, feel free to share with us what type of empath you are on any social media channels using #awakenedempath.

Intuitive Sensitivities

Apart from being a specific type of empath, you might also possess one or more of these intuitive sensitivities:

- **Clairvoyance:** The ability to visually receive information in the "mind's eye."
- **Clairaudience:** The ability to receive information through words and sounds not available in the immediate surroundings.
- **Clairsentience:** The ability to receive information through sensing subtle energy.
- **Clairgustance:** The ability to receive information from taste without putting anything in your mouth.
- **Clairscent:** The ability to receive information through scent that is not available in the immediate surroundings.
- **Clairtangency:** The ability to receive special information through touch.

You may wonder what the difference is between empathic abilities and intuitive sensitivities. The best way to distinguish them is by describing intuitive sensitivities as the medium through which you experience your empathic ability. Think of these intuitive sensitivities as a funnel through which you receive information.

For example, a fauna empath who can connect with the energy of animals might do so through clairsentience (clear sensing), but they might also communicate via clairtangency (touch). The psychometric empath, for instance, primarily experiences things through clairtangency (clear touch) but they might also may receive information through a vision (clairvoyance).

While all empaths have intuitive sensitivities, not all intuitive people are empaths. In other words, you can be born with an intuitive sensitivity without being an empath. However, almost all empaths possess at least one intuitive sensitivity, whether that be clairsentience, clairvoyance, clairaudience, or the other sensory-based "clairs."

Although it may not seem necessary to explore what type of intuitive sensitivity we have, it does help us go back to the origin root of how we absorb other people's energy and the energy of the surrounding environment. Simply asking yourself "What triggered this feeling or thought?" can help you develop more self-awareness when it comes to soaking up energy. Where you triggered by a thought, feeling, sound, scent, smell or taste? By exploring the origin of your inner energy, you will be able to better understand your gifts, use them skillfully, and work towards creating more balance in your life.

Chapter 2 – Empaths and Society

"Having a soft heart in a cruel world is courage, not weakness." – **Katherine Henson**

Your heartbeat is racing, your head is feeling foggy, and your body feels like a lifeless husk. It's 12pm, lunch time, and you've only just managed to take a breath of air. Around you, there is a steady buzz of energy clashing together like violent waves in the ocean. Like always, the emotional landscape around you feels heavy, oppressive, and frantic. In every direction, you can feel the anxiety, anger, lethargy and melancholy of the people you're surrounded by. You can also feel their excitement, enthusiasm, and bursts of hilarity. If the emotional landscape around you was painted by an artist, it would surely look like a deranged skirmish of blacks, blues, yellows and reds scattered everywhere. In fact, if you were to give a color to the energy you feel every day, it would likely be a murky brown or khaki: a combination of every shade of emotion savagely mixed together.

The reality is that for most empaths, each day feels like what I've just described. The fast-paced, breakneck speed of our lives means that we often barely know where we're standing, let alone how to cope with the tsunamis of energy constantly crashing into us. For most highly sensitive and empathic people, this constant onslaught of energy means one of three things: firstly, we caffeinate or drug ourselves and ignore our needs to keep up with society's demands. Second, we develop mental health issues such as anxiety and depression, and either keep forcing ourselves to be everything to everyone, or completely withdraw from society altogether. Or, third, we suppress and block out our sensitivity so deeply that we

20

appear to function like "normal" people — but inside, we develop serious chronic health issues.

These days, only a very small percentage of empaths learn how to embrace, use, and integrate their gifts into their daily lives.

But why? Why should only a few of us thrive, and the rest suffer? What is holding us back, and what can we do about it?

Childhood Wounds

"I spent many years trying to 'thicken my skin' and bury my feelings because as a child, some of my family members (who are not empaths, nor do they have empathy) shamed me into thinking I was too sensitive." – **Charlene, empath reader from lonerwolf.com**

As empaths, our inability to fully embody our gifts and function in a balanced way went all the way back to childhood, and even infancy.

As children, a great number of us were taught by our parents, carers, extended family members, and teachers, that showing any form of emotional vulnerability was "not OK." We were conditioned to believe that in order to be acceptable as human beings, we had to be like the other children. We were taught to "suck it up," "stop being cry babies," "get thicker skin," "stop being so sensitive" and go participate with the other kids, even if they overwhelmed us with their energy.

The truth is that many of us were taught to ignore and condemn our sensitivity because our parents, family members, and teachers didn't have the level of emotional maturity we

21

needed to thrive. Think about this for a moment: how emotionally intelligent were your parents? Did they openly express emotions such as sadness, fear, and even love and happiness in a balanced and healthy way? Or were they emotionally cold, out-of-touch with their feelings, or explosive and destructive?

Although it's tempting to blame our parents for our dysfunctional relationship with the world, it really isn't our parents fault. They too were likely victims of their upbringings. In fact, the emotional wounds we carry into adulthood are usually a product of inherited wounds that span back dozens, even hundreds, of generations.

In this way, we can see that our pain right now is actually a symptom of the collective pain we have inherited, and it is now up to us to embrace this opportunity to heal.

Social Conditioning

Our parents weren't the only ones who had a hand in our upbringing. If you want to understand why you have such a hard time flourishing in daily life, you need to understand how and why the society you're raised in influences you profoundly.

Since early childhood you are flooded with a barrage of images, stereotypes, ideals, and values from our society. You're taught that men should be strong, macho, and stoic, and possess only a limited array of emotions. You're taught that women should be sweet, sexy, stylish, bubbly, and an all-in-one solution to everyone's needs. And as a member of society, you're taught that you must be practical, efficient, successful, attractive, and socially desirable to fit in.

22

Usually, being socially desirable means being outgoing, entertaining, high-energy, and "thick" skinned. There is no room for gentleness, receptiveness or sensitivity at all in this equation. In fact, in the eyes of society, sensitivity is not only irrelevant, it's also an undesirable trait to have. Sensitivity equals being vulnerable, and being vulnerable equals danger. Why is sensitivity perceived as being dangerous? When we're sensitive, we feel things we were taught *not* to feel. When we're sensitive, we are completely open to attack. When we're sensitive, we are awake and in touch with our hearts – and *this* can be very threatening to the status quo indeed.

Common Empath Myths

Thanks to our childhood conditioning, it's not at all trendy or popular to be sensitive or feeling in a society that values efficiency, cold calculation, and industrial resilience. As a result, many of us are deeply misunderstood and hesitate to reveal our true selves for fear of being judged harshly. Even when we do reveal ourselves, we are often met with irritated, cold, or confounded emotional walls that fail to understand our needs. "Stop being so sensitive!" we might hear on a constant basis, or, "Calm down!"

One of the biggest struggles for us empaths in the 21st century is not only the fast-paced lifestyle we lead, but the misunderstanding of what sensitivity really is.

Here are some of the biggest myths out there that apply to empaths:

1. Being sensitive means being mentally ill.

As excellent listeners, confidants, and counsellors, we empaths tend to experience a lot of "emotional baggage dumping" from other people. As a result, we tend to accumulate large amounts of negative energy in our bodies and minds. Unfortunately, this energetic congestion can lead to a lot of lingering depressive and anxious emotions. Thus, on the surface, some of us may appear mentally ill (and sometimes, this might legitimately be the case). However, in most cases we're simply overburdened with emotional energy, kind of like our sinuses are during a cold or flu.

2. Sensitive is just another word for lazy.

In a world that values fast, efficient, and tireless work, there isn't much room for slowing down and listening to your inner self. It's no surprise then, that sensitive people are often seen as being "lazy." The pace at which we move in modern life inevitably leads to emotional, psychological, and even spiritual burnout. When our minds are constantly overloaded with stress, tension and pressure – as is the case with most empaths – the unavoidable result is energetic lethargy. This lethargy often translates to others as "dawdling around," "sitting on your bum," and wasting precious time.

How often have you suffered from things such as headaches, insomnia or chronic fatigue? These symptoms are almost always linked, in one way or another, to our unnaturally hurried state of living. In other words, as an empath, you're not lazy; you're simply exhausted. But other people struggle to truly understand this.

3. Sensitive people are emotionally weak.

The idea that sensitivity is a synonym for "weak" is just another one of the emotionally juvenile ideas we've been conditioned to believe. Men in particular are taught from a young age that showing emotions such as sadness is equivalent to being a "sissy." Somehow, society has developed the notion that being sensitive makes you "weak," when in fact it's the opposite: being sensitive makes you strong. Being sensitive opens you up to the world's pain and suffering, but also to the world's joy and beauty. Very few people have the courage to open their hearts enough to experiencing the world's pain as their own – to truly feel. This capacity to feel so deeply, when accepted and integrated consciously, is an immensely empowering gift. In fact, we could say that the only true "weakness" is shutting yourself off emotionally from the world and hiding behind a name, status, and job.

4. Sensitive people are melodramatic.

As children, most of us were taught early on to minimize ourselves and our needs in order to blend in with others and not draw "too much attention" to ourselves. Therefore, whenever we expressed our confusion, fear or feelings of being overwhelmed, it was common for our parents and even teachers to interpret this as "attention seeking." Eventually, as we grew up surrounded by emotionally immature people, we learned that any expression of emotion outside of the norm was a bad thing. So the more we expressed our true feelings, the more we were punished for being rebellious or were perceived as being melodramatic "actors."

As you can see, sensitivity has so much stigma surrounding it. It's no wonder that we struggle as empaths to feel comfortable with our gifts, let alone who we are at a core emotional and psychological level. Since childhood we were practically programmed to deny sensitivity, hide our emotions, pretend to be the same as others, and blend in with the crowd. Our oppressive social conditioning is precisely what makes it so difficult for us to thrive in healthy friendships and relationships.

Chapter 3 – Empath Friendships and Relationships

"I have people I don't even know come to me for help. I love helping people and everything but it's very shocking that I have complete strangers come to me for advice or any type of help." **– Danielle, empath reader from lonerwolf.com**

As highly sensitive people with the gift of compassion in our DNA, we naturally attract a lot of different types of people. Often, the people we tend to attract are deeply wounded individuals, making it difficult for us empaths to find authentically fulfilling relationships and friendships. How many times, for example, have strangers or people at work randomly opened their hearts to you and shared deeply intimate details of their lives? How many times have you been treated as an emotional dumping ground because of your caring and compassionate nature?

As you may already know, it's extremely hard to say "no" as an empath. As emotional radars, we instantly pick up the vibes around us and tend to gravitate the most to those are hurting – even if we're not in a good place. Our intense desire to help and soothe the pain of others often results in a whole range of interpersonal and inner issues. We need to learn how to establish healthy friendships and relationships if we're to thrive as empaths.

Empaths and Friendships

As empaths, we are loyal, attentive, and nurturing friends. We will stick by others through thick and thin. But if you're like

27

most empaths, you will tend to struggle with finding and maintaining friendships that are based on mutual giving, caring, and respect.

Because of our tendency to attract lost and wounded souls, we generally tend to wind up having one-sided, needy, and draining friendships. Having big hearts, we feel that it's against our nature to turn away those in need of help or an open and empathetic ear. The result is that we get sucked into exhausting, unfulfilling, and sometimes even narcissistic friendships.

Take one of our readers, Amanda, for example. Amanda related that one of the hardest things about university wasn't actually the study involved, but the people. Being highly empathic by nature, Amanda had made a number of friendships all based on the fact that she was an extremely empathic listener. But halfway through her course, she could tell that something was seriously wrong. Although she was popular, had a thriving social life, and was doing well in her studies, she felt completely depleted and was getting chronically sick. "It felt as though I had a thick layer of slime inside of me that never went away," she recalled. As she began to withdraw from her friends and focus only on her studies, she suddenly realized that the burden she was carrying was the emotional energy of her friends. After this realization, everything changed: "All the baggage I was carrying, it just went away. I felt new again. I felt this relief that I can only describe as inner lightness because I wasn't wasting my time on one-sided friendships. Finally, I was able to confirm that I am an empath."

As we can see, sometimes the best way to learn about taking care of ourselves as empaths is by creating distance and testing our hypothesis. However, sometimes it isn't possible for us to create distance. So, what do we do when there's no way to permanently distance ourselves?

One of the most useful empathic skills I learned was while working as an assistant in a large government building many years ago. At the time, I was surrounded by many people of all ages and races, and the atmosphere often felt thick and oppressive with undercurrents of tense stressful energy. As an empath, I knew that certain people there had serious emotional problems and struggles in their lives, even without being told so. Naturally, I couldn't help but gravitate towards these people and lend an open heart. But over time, I began feeling like I had dug myself into a very deep pit that I couldn't get out of. Every time I'd go to work, I would feel anxious, ungrounded, and extremely fatigued as a result of being near these people and engaging in deep conversations with them. The only problem was that, at the time, I was in debt, so quitting wasn't an option. Feeling desperate and stranded, I decided that my only option was to create emotional distance and focus on my job. While it was difficult at first to create emotional distance, eventually the people who had been unloading their energy on me got the message, and took a step back.

Thanks to learning this skill, I discovered how to create boundaries by respecting my needs for emotional "breathing space." Setting an emotional barrier is a good practice for those who have not learned how to deal with negative energy yet. So that you don't feel too emotionally isolated, you can also quietly send loving energy to those you wish to help but aren't in a position to.

In another chapter, you'll learn how to establish healthy boundaries and barriers along with many other empowering tools. But for now, here is a bit of advice if you're struggling as an empath with smothering friendships:

- Think about the friendships you have in your life in terms of emotional investments. Are you getting back what you give? Or are you giving more than you're getting?
- What percentage of time do you spend listening versus talking in your friendships? For example, you might listen 80% of the time, and only speak 20% of the time. If you find that you're listening more than sharing, you likely have an unhealthy and lopsided friendship on your hands.
- Experiment with staying away from your friends for the period of a week or two. How do you feel when their energy is not in your life? Do you feel more light and relaxed, or do you miss their company?
- Learn how to create emotional barriers by reclaiming your right to say "no." Saying no is not selfish; it is a sign that you care about yourself and your needs. In fact, learning how to say a gentle but firm "no" to others who are overstepping your boundaries is a form of self-love and respect. Although being assertive can feel weird and uncomfortable at first, keep practicing it. On average, it takes about 2 months to establish a new habit, so expect to feel a bit awkward at the beginning. However, if you persist, you'll savor the new freedom this skill gives you.
- If you struggle to say a flat out "no" to your friends, you might like to try saying "no thanks," "I'm not able to do that," "I can't, sorry," or other variations.

- If you're feeling overwhelmed by someone and their story, you can always take a time out. Trying breathing deep into your belly to ground yourself or make an excuse to leave (e.g. you have to catch the bus, meet a deadline, pick up the kids, etc.). In other chapters in this book, you'll learn more ways to ground yourself in social situations.
- If your friend/colleague is close to you, simply try openly communicating with them. For example, if you feel burdened by the story they're sharing you, you could tell them, "This is all a lot to absorb, I need time to take this in." Alternatively, you might even like to share with your close friends the fact that you're an empath and how this influences your relationship with energy.

After experimenting with these practices, you might discover that a significant number of your friends are actually "energy vampires" who take a lot from you but give very little in return. Don't worry, this is normal. While it might be difficult to let these people fade from your life, you'll be left with the few quality friendships that truly nourish and support you. Think of this process as a time of "purging" or detoxing your life. Almost every empath who has gone through this experience has come out feeling invigorated.

Empaths and Relationships

*"I can only connect deeply or not at all." – **Anaïs Nin***

One of the most beautiful and transcendental, but also gut wrenching, experiences empaths can ever go through is that of falling in love.

Love, to empaths, isn't just a shallow experience based on looks, social status or great sex. Instead, love is something that comes from the very heart and soul of what an empath is. Love is intense passion, unconditional devotion, and absolute fierce vulnerability. An empath loves and nurtures his or her family like nothing else in the world, and the beloved partner of an empath will receive a love so profound that it can be overwhelming.

When it comes to relationships, empaths truly shine. This is because it is not the face, body or personality of a person that empaths fall in love with, it is their Soul. Thus, in healthy and loving relationships, this translates to a deeply empathetic and almost telepathic understanding of the other, despite their flaws and shortcomings.

Because of their sacred gift of translating and embodying energy, empaths are able to spot their soulmates or twin flames a mile away. For example, without even knowing my partner Mateo, I was immediately able to see that we were energetically and spiritually compatible. Not only that, but I was able to intuitively sense that he would play a massive role in my life – and this was within moments of meeting him. Many empaths all over the world have encountered the same experience.

But the major drawback of having a big heart is that we often confuse love for pity. In other words, because we have a tendency to care deeply and strongly about others, we're often unable to differentiate the desire to help someone from the experience of loving someone. This struggle can often be seen in our tendency to get into unhealthy and codependent relationships. In fact, our habit of confusing love with pity is often why we end up attracting narcissists and other extremely disturbed people. We'll explore the empath-narcissist connection in a later chapter.

Drowning in the Ocean of Love

Beside getting into narcissistic and codependent relationships, we also have the tendency to *lose* ourselves in relationships. By losing ourselves, I mean that we tend to lose touch with our needs and often our sense of self.

There are a number of reasons why we lose touch with ourselves in relationships as empaths. The first is that we often become so focused on supporting, nurturing, and helping our partners (and children if we have them), that we become alienated from our own need to be taken care of. For years, sometimes decades, we become heavily enmeshed in the role of the caregiver, and to some extent it gives us a solid sense of identity. But the more we starve ourselves of love and attention, and channel that towards others, the harder it is for us to "keep it all together." In other words, we start experiencing emotional fatigue and inner neglect. We start falling apart.

The second reason why we tend to lose touch with ourselves in relationships is that we struggled to develop a strong individuated sense of self to begin with. Because we tend to feel constant emotions soaking into us from others, most of us empaths have grown up with a shaky sense of self. We're constantly left wondering, what energy is mine and what isn't? Why do I often feel like I'm travelling up and down on an emotional rollercoaster? Obviously, the more energetic input we've had from others, the harder it is for us to figure out who we truly are. Therefore, when we get into romantic relationships with others, it's very easy for us to "lose" ourselves, because we've always had a delicate sense of self.

Perhaps Eckhart Tolle put it the best when he says, "When you lose touch with yourself, you lose yourself in the world." As empaths, one of the quickest ways to completely lose our grounding in reality is by deferring our needs and wants in relationships.

Being Emotionally Smothered

Because of our tendency to lose ourselves in relationships, it is common for us to become attracted to emotionally unavailable people as a protection mechanism. We so often fall into dysfunctional cycles of pursuing people who cannot, or will not, grow close to us, thereby preventing us from being emotionally smothered or "trapped." This unconscious process of avoiding intimacy helps us to feel stable, but ends up backfiring on us once we realize that we need true, soulful intimacy. *— this makes a lot of sense*

As highly sensitive individuals, we simply cannot stand to feel trapped, constricted, or smothered in any way. We highly value our freedom and autonomy, making us particularly prone to staying single for long periods of time. In fact, it is essential that we experience breathing space in our relationships. Otherwise, we feel overwhelmed and inundated, not only by our partner's energy, but also by the constricting roles we have to play out. Our deep desire for autonomy and emotional breathing space is precisely why so many of us empaths tend to adopt unconventional relationships – and run away from those that don't allow such liberties. For example, some empaths I know prefer to sleep in different rooms from their partners, or even live in different houses. Others only see their partners once or twice a week or prefer long-distance relationships. Many empaths never choose to get married because of the energetic baggage marriage tends to create. For instance, I have never chosen to get married to my partner because I feel wonderfully secure in our relationship exactly as it is. The thought of being a "wife" makes me personally feel extremely uncomfortable and claustrophobic – the same goes for Mateo with the thought of being a "husband." Marriage just doesn't seem to suit us. However, not every empath feels this way, and that is fine too.

It is important that we identify our romantic needs as empaths. While some of these needs might be a little quirky or unusual, they are what help us to feel confident, stable, and happy in our relationships. Sometimes we need to release the stereotypes we carry in our heads of what relationships "should look like" and pay attention to what we actually want as sensitive people.

We also need to understand that our partners are not mind-readers, so we need to clearly identify our needs to create harmony in our relationships. Not only does identifying our needs create more romantic balance, but it also helps us to practice authenticity and self-love.

Here are some tips that can help you discover your romantic needs:

1. Explore your triggers.

When your needs are not met, you feel sadness, anger or disconnection towards your partner. Therefore, one of the best ways to uncover your needs is by exploring your emotional triggers, and the unmet needs hidden behind them. Explore your triggers by examining what made you react negatively: was it your own thoughts or behaviors that made you feel discomfort, or was it your partner's actions? It is important that you make this distinction so that you can take responsibility for your own actions, and help your partner to take responsibility for theirs. You also might like to note any situation that made you feel unhappy in the past, or is currently making you unhappy, to reflect on. I like to record my thoughts in online note-taking programs such as Evernote.

2. Distinguish between your needs and wants.

Your needs are very different from wants, so it is important that you make a clear distinction. While wants are surface desires that can easily change, needs are deep requirements that cannot be bargained with. When your wants are not met, you are prone to feeling annoyed and restless. But when your needs are not met, you feel depressed, resentful, misunderstood, displaced, and devalued. Needs are deal breakers: when they are not met, relationships quickly fizzle up and die.

In order to function well in a healthy relationship as an empath, you need to carefully distinguish between your deepest needs and superficial wants. To do this, ask yourself, "Would I still be happy in this relationship if I didn't get this?" For example, will you be happy in the long term with a partner who doesn't share your spirituality? Will you be happy in a relationship that doesn't involve a lot of sex? Will you be happy in a relationship that involves constant travel and little physical stability?

Remember, it's still important to share your wants with your partner, but needs are absolutely unbreakable – they are reflections of your values and requirements to thrive as a person.

3. Create your own Needs List.

Not knowing what your needs are in a relationship is like going to a grocery store without bringing a list. With no list, you'll be wandering through each aisle picking random items hoping they'll all help you cook something delicious. "Hmmm. Salt. Pickles. Cookies. Onions. Carrots. I sure hope all of these go well together!"

The same goes for relationships. You need to know what you're looking for before you commit, otherwise, you can easily fall into relationships that don't suit you. Even if you have already committed to someone, you will still benefit from exploring your needs and creating a Needs List.

A Needs List is exactly what it sounds like: a list of all the needs you require the most in the other person and the relationship. This list is a valuable tool that can help you pinpoint where your needs are not being met, and also whether a potential relationship will work or not.

Keep in mind that it's normal to feel a sense of uneasiness at the thought of creating a Needs List. This is because it will expose whatever is and isn't working in your relationship, and this reality can be confronting. But although the truth can be hard to face, it will provide you with the opportunity to either strengthen your current relationship, or help you find one that is more compatible with your needs. It is much more merciful to reach a clear conclusion about your relationship rather than to avoid the truth, drag everything out, and feel resentful about what is missing. Either way, you will receive a blessing in disguise.

Below you'll find a sample list with various needs. Feel free to draw inspiration from it to create your own list:

- I need regular physical affection
- I need to be physically attracted to my mate
- I need to feel safe sharing my feelings
- I need to feel safe sharing my thoughts
- I need a partner who shares the same values as me
- I need regular, honest communication
- I need someone who respects my space
- I need someone who will support my life goals
- I need daily private time away from my partner
- I need both of us to be monogamous
- I need a partner who will provide for my family
- I need a partner who isn't addicted to smoking, drugs, or alcohol
- I need us both to live together
- I need us to live apart
- I need a partner who shares the same spiritual beliefs
- I need a partner who keeps their promises
- I need a partner who does/doesn't want children
- I need a partner who is sensitive and empathetic
- I need a partner who accepts me just as I am
- I need someone with whom I can have deep conversations
- I need someone who wants to spend time with me each day
- I need us to both take equal initiative to uphold the relationship

You might also like to encourage your partner to create their own Needs List so that you can both work together to create mutual harmony and respect.

Also, try *not* to view this list as an ultimatum. In other words, if everything on this list isn't met then you will instantly terminate the relationship. Instead, pay attention to your partner's *willingness* to find ways to fulfill these needs – their openness is what counts!

4. Openly communicate your needs.

Sharing your needs with your partner can be uncomfortable and awkward, especially if you haven't had practice. As empaths, many of us tend to favor our partner's needs in place of our own. So it can feel strange to finally share our own needs and speak up! But once you get over the initial discomfort, you will find your relationship becoming deeper, richer, and more rewarding.

In order to openly communicate your needs, you need to carefully pick a time in which both of you are relaxed and available. Otherwise, if you pick the wrong time your partner might feel overwhelmed and inundated.

When you start communicating with your partner, try to pick one need at a time, starting with what you need the most. For example, you might need to spend time snuggling with them every day because you aren't getting enough physical contact. Explain to your partner your need in a casual and sincere way. For example, "You know, I would really love to cuddle with you in the afternoon. I need to feel closer with you. What do you think?" If your need revolves around something they're doing which is intensely unsettling to you, e.g. outbursts of anger, try to approach this delicately. [Instead of saying that there is something wrong with them or the relationship, tell them what you need.] When you communicate in a way that suggests you are blaming them, they will be more prone to shutting off and becoming defensive. To keep the dialogue between the two of you open, try to phrase what you say positively, not negatively. For example, if your partner has angry outbursts, you might say, "I had something on my mind that I wanted to share with you. When you get angry, I feel threatened and overwhelmed. I need to feel safe around you to feel comfortable in this relationship. I would love us to both work through the problems you're experiencing so we can enjoy more peace."

By sharing how you feel and proposing a solution, your chances of having your needs met and enhancing your relationship will increase.

5. Take responsibility for your happiness.

[Finally, it's important to take responsibility for your happiness. True happiness comes from within, not from the external world, or even from your partner. While it's important to have a relationship that meets your needs, your happiness shouldn't be dependent on your relationship.] I have mentored one too many people who have based all of their happiness on how successfully they're doing in the romance realm. Once their relationship fails, or if they continue to remain single, they become depressed, bitter, and angry. It's dangerous to base our happiness on something as unpredictable and external as a relationship. Even if that relationship feels secure, we never truly know what will happen.

It is also unfair to expect our partners to make us happy because that places an immense psychological and emotional

40

burden on them. Not only are they responsible for finding their own fulfillment, but they're also responsible for making *us* feel fulfilled as well. Through time, pressure, tension, stress, and resentment slowly build as one or both partners start to feel more like cell mates rather than soulmates. Relationships like this that have the "You must make me happy" dynamic are very unhealthy and often end up failing. However, relationships that have a "Let's be happy together" dynamic, in which each person takes responsibility for their own happiness, tend to last.

The difference between the "You must make me happy" dynamic and sharing our needs is the intention. When we share our needs out of the belief that our *partners* are responsible for our happiness, we inevitably suffer over and over again. However, when we share our needs out of respect for ourselves, we take responsibility for our own happiness.

Been there.. now Iknow

One of the best things my own partner ever said to me was, "I want you to support me, not try to complete me."

Empaths and Sexuality

One of the most intense experiences of energy exchange we can ever experience as empaths is during our sexual encounters. As we have the tendency to soak up and internalize the energy of others, physical contact makes this process more extreme. For example, have you ever found yourself absorbing your partner's feelings of agitation, anger or even anxiety during lovemaking? Do you feel tired, heavy or moody after getting intimate?

However, sex can also be an intensely euphoric and erotic experience for us empaths. Because we mirror our partner's feelings (and even sensations), we often get double the pleasure, making sex a truly mind blowing experience!

When it comes to sex, we need to clearly explore our needs. For example, most empaths don't like one night stands or meaningless sex because it not only takes a lot of energy, but also feels too faceless and shallow. As sensitive people, we tend to prefer having sex with people who we are emotionally connected to because we value sex as being a sacred act. So ask yourself, what are your needs and values? When is sex permissible for you: on the first date, within the first week, or once you have committed to a relationship? Don't be afraid to set boundaries and honor your energy: you should never feel pressured to have sex, and if you do, run the other direction!

As a highly sensual being, you might also like to explore your likes and dislikes surrounding sex. Remember that your partner isn't a mind reader! So explore how you like to be touched, and have a frank discussion with your beloved. Your needs matter too.

Empaths and Dating

It is an understatement to say that dating is difficult as an empath. With all of the swirling energy, desire, and emotions to navigate and sort through, this time can be confusing and overwhelming.
One of the easiest ways to discover if someone is compatible with you is to gauge their emotional intelligence. Are they a kind and sensitive person? Will they be respectful towards your sensitivities? Or are they emotionally stunted? Remember, we tend to attract narcissistic types who lack empathy (more on that in another chapter)! So be aware.

Screening your dates can be a fun and revealing process. You can use the following points to determine the suitability of your date.

SENSITIVITY IQ CHECKLIST

- Do they pay attention to what you're saying?
- Do they show sincere concern about you or other people?
- Do they respect your boundaries?
- Do they remember details about your life?
- Do they have any interests that involve caring for someone or something (like nature or a world event)?
- Do they seem emotionally secure and balanced?
- Do they take responsibility for their actions?
- Are they comfortable with meaningful conversation?
- Are they attentive to your needs?
- Are they in tune with their own needs and dreams?

Seven to ten "yeses" means that your date has high sensitivity – which is wonderful.

Three to six "yeses" means your date has a moderate sensitivity IQ – which is OK.

Zero to three "yeses" means your date has a very low sensitivity IQ – which is a red flag and you'd be better off finding someone more emotionally aware.

As always, pay attention to your instincts when you are dating. What does your intuition tell you about the other person? Does something feel "off" about them, even though they are externally charming? Do their words match their energy? As an empath, you're prone to freezing around inauthentic people. Do yourself a favor and pay close attention to your gut feelings.

43

Finding an Emotionally Compatible Partner

With so many different types of people in the world, which ones make the best partners for us as empaths? From what I have observed, there are three main types of emotionally compatible partners for sensitive people. Your ideal "type" will be completely unique to your personality, values, and needs. Pay attention to these qualities in the people you date and see how you react to each temperament. You can also use this list as a fun way of classifying your current partner and learning how to interact with them in a deeper way.

1. The Strong Silent Type

This type of partner is forbearing, trustworthy, consistent, and stable, meaning that you can depend on them no matter what. The Strong Silent Type (SST) is an extremely grounded type of person. SSTs provide empaths with a solid foundation and a shoulder to lean on in tough times. In a sense, SSTs and Empaths are opposites who balance each other out wonderfully. On one hand, empaths learn how to be more emotionally grounded from their SST partners, and SSTs learn how to express their emotions more openly. The Strong Silent Type is an ideal partner for empaths as they are loyal, tolerant, and dependable.

Here are some tips on how to enhance your connection with your SST partner:

- Agree to make more physical contact. SSTs are not overly conscientious in the affection realm and may need a bit of guidance and suggestion. Discuss with them how much you enjoy hugs, kisses, cuddles, and intimate time because it helps you to feel close with them.

- Ask your SST partner how they feel. Sharing feelings with each other, even if it is difficult for the SST, deepens your emotional bond.
- Express your gratitude through words and actions. SSTs usually express their love through acts of service. By doing something kind and thoughtful for your SST partner, you will show them how much you care. Also, voicing your appreciation for them helps them feel affirmed.
- Find a physical hobby to share. SSTs are earth people who enjoy practical activities. By sharing a mutual physical activity, you will both grow closer together.

2. The Thinker

Thinkers process the world primarily through logic and reason. As highly intelligent people, Thinkers love absorbing new information and solving problems. When coupled with an empath partner, the Thinker's rational approach to life helps the empath to experience emotional and mental clarity. Thinkers are also levelheaded and stay cool in times of crisis; however, they do tend to favor the head over the heart and ignore their own emotions.

Here are some tips that will help you to enhance your connection with your Thinker partner:

- Learn how to articulate what you're feeling. Thinkers struggle to interpret emotions that are not expressed in a way they can understand. When you're feeling upset or burdened with energy, clearly articulate to your partner what is happening to you.

- Ask for help when you need it. Thinkers show their love and concern for you through problem-solving. When you are feeling lost or in a rut, open your heart and ask for assistance. Your Thinker partner will feel happy and valued when you ask them, even if they don't openly express it. Thinkers will always be able to find a solution as long as they have enough information.
- Share one problem at a time. Don't dump all of your struggles onto Thinkers at once, because this can mentally inundate them. Pick one clear problem at a time. If you have possible solutions, share them with your Thinker partner as well for feedback – they love giving practical advice.
- Spend time together each day. Make sure you express how important affection and physical contact is for you. Mutually agree on a time where you can forget the world and unwind together. Regular closeness will enhance your connection.
- Remember that you both speak very different "languages." Sometimes miscommunication happens between Thinkers and empaths because both function in such different ways. Keep in mind that Thinkers approach life with a rational, logical, and problem-solving mindset. On the other hand, you as an empath tend to approach life with an emotional, intuitive, and feelings-based mindset. If you feel like your Thinker partner is focusing too much on "fixing" your issue rather than empathizing with you, share that with them. Be open about your feelings and needs because they can't read your mind.

3. The Empath

Other empaths can make amazing partners, especially because they meet you on the same wavelength. When two empaths get into a relationship, the passion and love both experience can be mind-blowing. Because each partner can feel the other's energy, any emotion is quadrupled and amplified. However, while empaths can make compassionate and supportive partners, there is also the risk of being overwhelmed. Two stressed out empaths in a relationship can put everything out of balance very quickly. In order to maintain harmony, each partner needs to set clear boundaries and express their needs clearly.

Here are some tips on how to enhance your connection with your empath partner:

- Spend time alone. Both of you need to spend time alone separately in order to neutralize yourselves. When you spend too much time together, there is the tendency to feed off each other's emotional energy, which can result in experiencing overwhelming feelings of anxiety, irritability, fatigue, etc. Spending time alone is absolutely imperative as it will help you to relax and find inner harmony.
- Stay grounded. As both of you are emotion-oriented people, there is a tendency to lose connection from grounded, physical reality. In order to maintain balance, find activities to do together that are grounding. For example, you might like to take walks in nature together, cook together, make art together, take up a sport hobby, etc.
- Set clear boundaries. As I mentioned earlier, it's easy for us to "lose ourselves" in our relationships, and this also applies to relationships with other empaths. Ensure that you identify your needs in the relationship

47

and learn how to maintain your own individuated sense of self. For example, setting boundaries might mean choosing not to sleep in the same room as your partner or maintaining friends outside of the relationship. It can be very easy for two empaths to become completely enmeshed, which is unhealthy. Boundaries must be established.

Finally, keep in mind that certain people can overlap all three types of partners. For example, I consider my partner to be a mixture of the Thinker, the Strong Silent Type, and the Empath, because he has a very balanced emotional and logical brain. However, some people share more in common with a single type, and that's normal too.

By learning what types of partner suit you the best, you can learn how to fine-tune your quest to find a mate, or interact more smoothly with the one you already have.

Empaths, Soulmates and Twin Flames

Sometimes it takes us many relationships to find a person who is truly compatible with us. When we find our soulmates or twin flames, it is usually after we have gone through a lot of psychological maturation and life experience. Even still, our soulmates or twin flames sometimes appear in our lives at the most inopportune or unexpected times.

What role do Soulmates and Twin Flames play in an empath's life? Quite simply, Soulmates and Twin Flames are the people in our lives who are emotionally, mentally, and spiritually compatible with us. But what's the difference between the two?

Soulmates can be thought of as the people in our lives who offer their unconditional support, love, and companionship to us. Twin Flames, on the other hand, are people who aid our Souls in spiritual transformation and growth. While Soulmates are people we're completely comfortable and familiar with on a Soul level, Twin Flames are people who challenge us, mirror us, and help us to transform into the people we're destined to become.

If you've found your Soulmate as an empath, you'll feel as though:

- They're your best and truest friend
- You can share all of your deepest inner self with them
- You're completely safe and secure with them
- You share the same dreams and values
- You experience complete energetic harmony together

Soulmates can be romantic or platonic. Not only that, but you can have many soulmates throughout your lifetime.

On the other hand, if you've found your Twin Flame as an empath, you'll feel as though:

- You both embody the yin and yang (you are the opposite, but also the same)
- They mirror your best and worst attributes
- You can be your authentic self and share anything with them
- You both challenge each other in ways that can be uncomfortable and scary, but beneficial
- You are both catalysts for each other's spiritual growth

- The connection you have is intense and can easily burn out when not balanced properly
- You both feel driven towards a higher purpose

As the name suggests, we only have one "Twin" Flame, and the connection is almost always romantic.

If you're looking for your Soulmate or Twin Flame, it's essential that you first learn how to take care of yourself. Your search will be easier when you learn how to heal your unresolved inner wounds, develop a strong sense of self, and be grounded in self-love. In the second half of this book, you'll find practices that can help you accomplish this balanced state.

Finally, a big issue that some empaths face is unrequited love and all the grief that accompanies this experience. If someone truly is your soulmate or twin flame, the relationship will happen sooner or later. Don't put your life on hold for another person, no matter how badly you want to be with them. If it's meant to be, it will be.

Advice For Empaths in Relationships

As empaths we feel everything our partners feel. When they're sad, we feel distraught. When they're depressed, we feel weighed down with inner heaviness. But when they feel joy and excitement, we also feel that same sense of elation which is enhanced by our love for them. Indeed, our relationships are fundamentally *intense*. The highs are very high, and the lows are very low.

If you're needing a little bit of guidance in your relationships, you might find the following bits of empath-tailored advice useful:

- **If you're feeling overwhelmed in your relationship**, dedicate some time to journal or mentally explore these feelings and ask "why"? Then, take a step back and examine how you can both mutually create balance and relaxed energy together.
- **If you're feeling a lack of connection in your relationship**, try to create a ritual you can carry out every day with your partner that is mutually satisfying. If the feeling persists, explore the places where you are compatible and incompatible. It's OK to feel as though you or your partner have changed across the course of your relationship. People grow, and sometimes they grow apart. It's important that you explore this possibility, but also look into ways to deepen your connection if you still have the spark.
- **If you're feeling as though you've lost yourself in your relationship**, think back to what you enjoyed doing before you entered your partnership. What did you once do that brought you a lot of satisfaction that you have since given up? For example, you may have enjoyed painting, meditating, eating certain types of food, going out with friends, spending time in nature or being around animals. Try to slowly incorporate these activities into your life. You can also regularly keep a journal or scrapbook of your dreams, desires, feelings, and thoughts – this will help you to fall back into your sense of self again.
- **If you feel emotionally unstable in your relationship**, ask yourself, what feelings are mine, and what feelings are my partners? Try to trace your

emotions back to thoughts; for example, were you thinking anything in particular when a certain emotion overcame you? Or did the emotion come spontaneously without any internal stimuli? Start paying attention to your thinking patterns and hormonal fluctuations, and be as objective as you can.

- **If you're feeling doubtful about your relationship,** write, draw out or brainstorm your feelings on a piece of paper. On one side, explore all the good things about your relationship, and on the other side, explore all the bad things. Weigh up both sides, and reflect on the overall state of your relationship. You can also ask yourself important questions such as, "Does my partner share my values and beliefs?" "Are these problems shallow grievances or deep issues?" "Does my partner treat me with the love, care, respect, and consideration I deserve?" "Am I sacrificing things that make me happy in order to be in this relationship?" "Is it possible to solve any of these issues together?"

Often, all we really need as empaths is a little time to take a step back, breathe, and reflect. As highly intuitive people, it is important that we trust our gut feelings above all else when it comes to relationships. By reflecting on and practicing the information mentioned in this chapter, you'll be able to find more serenity in your friendships and relationships.

Chapter 4 – Empaths and the Workplace

"Aside from finding it near impossible to hold a job in a social environment, I find it hard to decipher the difference between my feelings and emotions, and someone else's. Its often led me to be a loner, hibernating for long periods of time." – **Monica, empath reader at lonerwolf.com**

The workplace can be a place of great joy and self-fulfillment or a place of intense stress and emotional overload for empaths. So it makes sense that we should think very carefully about our career choices.

In the right environment, we flourish, feel energized, and contribute our gifts to this planet. Because we are artists, healers, visionaries, and inventors at heart, we need to choose careers that satisfy our desire to give and nurture. We thrive in jobs that are multi-layered, flexible, and varied because we get bored very easily of restrictive environments.

The very worst environments for us to work in are those with little privacy, too many people, and aggressive work politics. We tend to wither in jobs that require us to constantly be "switched on" or those that are fueled by adrenaline and competition. Examples of jobs we don't generally thrive in include those in the military, police force, government, law, customer service, and large corporations. Any job that requires a lot of physical energy, pressure or conflict are generally not good matches for us.

On the other hand, we tend to be well suited to the following types of jobs:

53

- Landscaping
- Gardening
- Forestry
- Environmental protection
- Graphic design
- Blogging
- Writing
- Artist
- Musician
- Editor
- Librarian
- Self-employed business owner
- Social worker
- Life coach
- Massage therapist
- Clergy
- Non-profit work
- Virtual assistant
- Animal rescue
- Veterinary medicine
- Hospice work
- Psychotherapist
- Psychologist
- Physical therapy
- Art therapy
- Alternative medicine practitioner
- Social work
- Fitness instructor
- Yoga or pilates teacher
- Meditation teacher
- Nurse
- Physician
- School teacher

- University professor
- Marriage counsellor

There are so many wonderful jobs out there for empaths, and this list is by no means exhaustive. As you can see, we tend to thrive in the artistic, environmental, academic, humanitarian, and healing professions. However, in order to thrive in these fields, we need to learn how to preserve our energy, set boundaries, and take care of ourselves.

Compassion Fatigue

One of the greatest struggles we tend to experience in the work environment is something called compassion fatigue.

Compassion fatigue is an emotional state of burnout that occurs in highly demanding healing professions such as medicine, social work, law, and psychotherapy. Empaths who work in fields such as these tend to suffer from the highest degree of compassion fatigue because of their tendency to absorb their client's stressful emotions. If you have experienced, or are currently experiencing, compassion fatigue, you will struggle with problems such as anxiety, fatigue, self-contempt, insomnia, weight problems, chronic illness, depersonalization or even depression.

It's vital that we learn how to practice self-care, especially if we work in fields that demand a lot of empathy and energy. If you think you might be struggling with this problem, or are at risk, incorporate the following practices into your life:

1. Take care of your physical needs.

No matter how demanding your job is, make sure you take care of yourself. Don't skip meals, avoid exercise, or stay up too late. Ensure that you eat regular, nutritionally rich meals, exercise every day for at least twenty minutes, and set a regular bedtime. Getting eight hours of sleep as an empath is absolutely vital for your nervous system to unwind and recover.

2. Plan regular breaks.

Make sure you sprinkle multiple breaks throughout your day so that you don't overwork yourself. In your breaks, make a cup of tea, go outside, breathe in fresh air, or spend time meditating. If you can, take a small power nap for ten to twenty minutes.

3. Engage in outside hobbies.

Don't let your work be your only passion. Find other enjoyable activities that are outside of your profession. For example, you might like to join a book club, take up a craft, or join a local interest group. As a writer and mentor, I like to have "no internet, no people" days where I can disconnect from my duties and do something relaxing like walking in nature, doing yoga or creating artwork. By engaging in outside hobbies, you will create more work-life balance, which is essential to your wellbeing.

4. Express your emotions.

If you're feeling inundated and burned out, find a way to express your emotions. You might like to keep a journal and record your thoughts or share your feelings with your friend or partner. By expressing your emotions, you will energetically release them from your body, making you feel much better.

yes need this!!

56

5. Practice relaxation techniques.

Learn how to be mindful of your compassion fatigue and ensure that you make time to unwind. Use techniques such as meditation, progressive muscle relaxation, deep breathing, and exercise to calm your body. Take soothing baths with epsom salts, get massages from your partner or a health professional, and listen to calming music.

6. Learn when to draw the line.

Your time, health, and energy is important too. Learn to compassionately say "no" to demanding or negative people who are encroaching on your energy boundaries. Remember that in order to truly care for others you must first care for your own needs.

I'll expand on a variety of other practices later on in this book which will help you to preserve your energy and create more inner balance.

How to Thrive in Your Workplace

One of the worst experiences we can go through as sensitive people is the feeling of being devalued and crushed in our workplaces. We function the best when we are in supportive, laidback, and friendly environments. However, unfortunately we don't always find ourselves in the most ideal jobs. If you're currently in a job that stresses you out, consider the following tips which might make your workdays easier as an empath.

1. Create a serenity bubble.

If you feel stressed out at work, try creating a serenity bubble around your workstation. Decorate your space with objects that soothe you and remind you of the outside world, such as flowers, crystals, statues, inspiring posters, sacred objects, mementos, and so forth. You might even like to place photos of your loved ones around your space to infuse it with loving energy.

2. Stay organized.

Cluttered, messy, and chaotic environments create feelings of claustrophobia, confusion, and anxiety. There is a reason why "cleanliness is next to godliness." When we have clean and organized environments, we find it easier to stay grounded, mindful, focused, and relaxed. Try to keep your workspace orderly and free from rubbish, hoarded items, and clutter. Notice how much more calm you feel when everything is orderly.

3. Plan ahead.

Avoid traffic jams, busy highways, and the morning rush by planning ahead. Make your meals ahead of time, plan your trips, and give yourself enough time in the morning to go slowly at your own pace. By planning ahead, you won't feel as much dread surrounding going to work.

4. Define your boundaries.

Are you interested in making friends at your job, or are you just there to do your work? Do you want people calling you on your days off, or do you want privacy? Are you comfortable with attending afterwork parties and get-togethers, or do you want to go home to your family? Empaths are prone to getting sucked into draining and extraneous social commitments at work. Think about what *you* need the most and clearly define your boundaries. If you don't want to get emotionally involved with others, stay to yourself, and find joy simply focusing on your job. You are allowed to listen to your own needs, so don't let others pressure you.

5. Prepare for emotional contagion.

As we'll further explore in the next chapter, emotional contagion is our tendency to unconsciously mirror and take on the emotions of those around us. In workplaces that operate in confined spaces, emotional contagion can be particularly intense. In order to handle emotional contagion, be mindful of the energy in your workplace first thing in the morning. Also try tuning into the energy at various times of the day, say, on your tea breaks. If the energy feels dense, consciously breathe and ground yourself through your senses. Keep your body language open so that you don't mirror other's emotions. If you are allowed, put on quiet and calming music. If all else fails, go to the toilet for a few minutes to gather yourself. (One of my favorite refuges in the past has been toilet cubicles!) *or Breaks in the car.*

6. Keep your conversations factual.

To avoid getting sucked into the drama of energy vampires, keep your conversations as factual as possible. Be aware that energy vampires thrive on your reactions and responses, so be as neutral as possible if they try to involve you, and keep the conversations short.

7. Work remotely.

If you have the option, try asking your boss or supervisor if it's possible to work from your home. Many jobs these days provide work-from-home arrangements where you can use online tools such as skype, google documents, and Trello to fulfill your job. Try to ask your boss for a trial of two days a week so that you can both ease into the arrangement. Make sure you build a good case that highlights all the benefits *they* will experience!

8. Develop an escape plan.

If all else fails and you desperately want to leave your job, develop an escape plan. Sometimes it isn't always possible to leave right away, especially if you have no other jobs lined up. Form your escape plan by updating your resume, saving extra money, and hunting out prospective jobs that will suit your empathic sensibilities. You might even like to take a course to enhance your skillset.

Personally, when I discovered that my jobs were making me sick, it became my single-minded mission to find work that fulfilled me and matched my empath temperament. According to the World Health Organization, we spend one third of our adult lives working – *one third*![1] So it should be right at the top of our priority list to find jobs that we love doing. Life is too short to spend time in a job you despise.

Self-Employment

Self-employment is one of the best options for us as empaths, and no wonder, since there are so many perks! Not only do you get to set your own hours and be your own boss, but you also get to work from the comfort of your own home, experience variety, and actualize your dreams. One of the most demoralizing experiences is to feel devalued and taken for granted, especially when you have so much to offer this planet. As one empath shared with me, "I felt like I was making zero impact in my corporate job … it was like pieces of my soul were dying little by little. Now I wake up and my soul is happy, vibrant, and finally free. Even though I'm not making as much money, I'm doing what I love, and that is what ultimately counts."

Empaths function particularly well when they are self-employed. We excel as entrepreneurs, freelance designers, editors, writers, seamstresses, independent contractors, consultants … you name it! We are free spirits, so we need as much space to breathe and be autonomous as possible.

As a self-employed empath, I want to share with you some of the best tips that I've gathered across the years, which will help you to establish your own business (if you feel drawn to doing this):

- Think about your talents and strengths: what are you gifted at doing?
- Explore what you are drawn to over and over again – this will be your passion.
- See if there's a market or "niche" for your passion by researching online.
- Ask yourself, "What do I want to change the most in this world?" Think big, not small.
- Use the power of social media to boost and popularize your business.
- Sign up to a course or read books about how to build your own business.
- Brainstorm and record all of your ideas.

- When in doubt, consult your intuition or gut feelings by asking, "is this the right decision?" Whatever strong and clear response arises in your body is the answer.
- Think about how much time you can dedicate to your business, and create boundaries so that you have a work-life balance.
- Set small and easy goals to accomplish step by step.
- Create an organized schedule for each working day.
- Keep affirming that it's OK to make a living doing what you love!
- Separate your living space from your work space to increase productivity (this is important).
- Be cautious of burnout when you first start your business. Take regular breaks and look after your physical and emotional needs.
- Remember that there is no such thing as "failure" – only lessons to learn from!

Finally, keep in mind that self-employment is very different from typical employment. As an empath it's important that you go slowly and explore what you truly want, need, and value to make working for yourself worthwhile. Being your own boss can be overwhelming at first, but with clear goals, objectives, and a plan in place, you'll be able to create the job of your dreams.

In the next few chapters we'll explore what science, psychology, shamanism, and mysticism have to say about being an empath. After these four chapters, we'll then move onto the more practical parts of this book which include exploring topics such as the shadow self, narcissists, energy vampires, empath parenting, the spiritual awakening process, and healing on the physical, emotional, mental, and spiritual levels as an empath.

Chapter 5 – The Psychological Understanding of Being an Empath

The notion of being an empath is not just a fluffy new age belief. It has a real psychological and scientific basis.

When I first discovered that I had empathic abilities, it took me a long time to fully accept that I was a little different from others. For many years I resisted and ignored the fact that I was extremely receptive to the subtle undercurrents of energy all around me. Because I mistrusted all the empath jargon I heard, my natural inner cynic took over and ran the show. I'm sure, at some point, you've experienced what it's like to have that nagging feeling of doubt and skepticism in the back of your brain! It wasn't until I started developing a stronger connection to my Soul that I realized that I could genuinely feel the emotional energy of others as my own. The more internally balanced I became, the clearer I could see that a lot of the anxiety I experienced was a result of the emotional "soundtracks" playing around me that I could pick up on, often without even consciously registering it.

Two of the biggest discoveries I made that helped me to embrace the fact that I was an empath were found in the fields of psychology and science. In this chapter, we'll explore the psychological basis of being an empath, and in the next chapter, the scientific understanding.

Emotional Contagion

As children, we were biologically wired to interpret the emotional climate around us. Without learning how to tune into the emotions of others, we never would have been able to survive our evolutionary growth. For example, how could a mother feed her child without interpreting its emotions? Similarly, how could a tribe protect their village without understanding the emotions of those approaching them?

One of the ways in which we learned how to feel close to others was through a process known as emotional contagion. Emotional contagion is the psychological term that describes our tendency to unconsciously mirror the facial expressions, sounds, postures, and movements of others. Psychoanalyst Gerald Schoenewolf describes emotional contagion as the "process in which a person or group influences the behavior of another person or group through the conscious or unconscious induction of emotional states and behavioral attitudes."[1] In other words, it is actually possible for us to be infected by the emotions of others (and vice versa).

Emotional contagion is a form of unconscious mimicry that begins in infancy, often within minutes of being born.[2] As we grow, we continue to experience emotional contagion all throughout our lives, often without even knowing it. For example, have you ever felt completely fine before going to work, but within a few minutes around others, felt terribly unhappy? Or have you ever walked into a busy shopping center relaxed, and walked out anxious and flustered? These are both common examples of emotional contagion.

Emotional contagion can happen at an individual level all the way up to a group or even national level. For example, in an experiment conducted by researcher Sigal Barsade in a business school, students were divided into small groups. In each group, an actor was hired to convey one of four different moods: cheerful enthusiasm, serene warmth, hostile irritability, and depressed sluggishness.[3]

What Barsade found was interesting: the groups with the actor that conveyed positive emotions showed a notable increase in good mood, less conflict, more cooperation, and better overall results compared to the negative groups.

The fact is that facial expressions, tones of voice, and body movements all convey meaning or energy. When we unconsciously mirror the expressions, tones, and movements of others, we're immediately able to access the emotional states of those around us. Not only does the discovery of emotional contagion help us to understand our empathic gifts, but it also sheds insight into why we "have little choice" in what type of energy we receive. Because emotional contagion is a very primal, biological process that occurs subconsciously, it is impossible for us to filter what we receive. But this limitation doesn't mean that we have to suffer. In fact, with the right tools, we can learn how to release the emotions we feel from others, and become empowered beings again. Not only that, but it's also possible to shift the energy we send into the world, and therefore positively influence those around us. We'll explore how to do this in later chapters.

For now, here are some quick tips that will help you reduce the effects of emotional contagion on your psyche:

- Reduce eye contact with people who emanate "heavy" vibrations
- Limit your contact with very negative people and create physical distance

- If you can't limit your contact with negative people, focus on breathing deeply from your belly when around them
- Stay grounded through mindfulness
- Be conscious of your tendency to mirror other people's body language and tones of voice
- Adjust your own body language so you portray openness and positivity (this will have an uplifting psychological effect on you)
- Try to stick to small talk or light topics of conversation

But the question still remains: if we were all born with the ability to experience emotional contagion, why isn't everyone an empath?

There are a number of possible reasons why experiencing emotional contagion doesn't always lead to being an empath. The first reason is that empaths simply have a higher emotional sensitivity and receptivity to other people's emotions. In other words, while most people can see and understand a small range of emotional cues, empaths can perceive the full spectrum of emotional colors.

The second reason could be that empaths are more open to understanding and relating to others than most people. While we all have the capacity to be empaths, this gift is often locked away due to early childhood and adolescent trauma, making it difficult for most people to mirror others. If you've ever experienced an intense amount of suffering in your life, you'll know how hard it is to show interest in others on a conscious or subconscious level. Therefore, emotional contagion is less intense for those in our society who have repressed or numbed their sensitivity.

Thanks to emotional contagion, we understand that our empathic gifts are a result of unconsciously mirroring the energy of others. In other words, we often automatically *feel* a person's emotions before we can intellectually process what is happening to us or even know where the feeling came from.

But there is another piece to the puzzle when it comes to understanding why we have empathic gifts, and that is science's discovery of mirror neurons.

Chapter 6 – The Scientific Understanding of Being an Empath

*"A human being is a part of the whole, called by us 'Universe,' a part limited in time and space. He experiences himself, his thoughts and feelings as something separate from the rest—a kind of optical delusion of his consciousness. The striving to free oneself from this delusion is the one issue of true religion. Not to nourish it but to try to overcome it is the way to reach the attainable measure of peace of mind." – **Albert Einstein**[1]*

Recently, science has finally begun to catch up to the knowledge and wisdom that Buddhism, Hinduism, Shamanism, Taoism and many other mystical cultures have known all along: that *everything is linked to everything else, and, at the deepest level, all is One.*

This view seems to be increasingly confirmed by modern science, especially by quantum physics through "*Quantum Entanglement.*" This is a field that is far too complex for this book, but essentially it is when two particles are in the same place and can instantly communicate with each other no matter what the distance is. This theory may describe why we as empaths can sometimes sense or feel things from others who aren't even in the same vicinity as us. If you have ever felt or "known" something about a loved one who lives in another city or country to you, you'll understand what I mean.

In this chapter, we'll explore the solid scientific basis that underpins what it means to be an empath. I'll share with you some fascinating experiments and examples that will help you to understand science's perspective on your amazing gift.

Mirror Neurons

Although science has yet a long way to go to explain our empathic gifts, there has been a lot of exciting research into the field of empathy, and the most important discovery has occurred in the field of neuroscience. This discovery has been called *Mirror Neurons*, and they play a significant role in our ability to perceive other's emotions as our own.[2]

One of the most famous mirror neuron studies was conducted in the late 1980's when a group of Italian neuroscientists placed electrodes in the inferior frontal cortex of macaque monkey's brains in order to study the neurons dedicated to controlling hand movements. This led to the astonishing observation that some of the neurons in the monkeys mirrored the neurons within humans when the monkey's saw the humans pick up a piece of food, as if *the monkeys* were getting the food themselves.

This discovery introduced science to the idea of mirror neurons, which are understood as nerve cells in our brains that are triggered by imitation as a way of learning, understanding, and empathizing in social situations.

We've all experienced the mirror neurons within us firing up at one time or another in our lives. Have you ever seen someone accidentally prick themselves with a sharp object, bite their tongue or bumped their head, and cringed in pain yourself? Or have you ever witnessed someone burn their hand or get hit in the groin, and wince as though *you* were experiencing their pain? These experiences were all products of your mirror neurons being activated.

Essentially, these "smart cells" within our brains understand the context of other people's experiences. Once fired up, they help us to bring meaning and understanding to the actions of others. For this reason, mirror neurons can actually distinguish your intention; in other words, they "know what you are thinking" according to neuroscientist Marco Iacoboni.[3]

Interestingly, it is also possible for our mirror neurons to not work properly. For example, professor Vilayanur S. Ramachandran, a neuroscientist from the University of California, released in the 1990's a controversial hypothesis known as the "Broken Mirror." In it, Ramachandran provides compelling evidence that people with autism have dysfunctional or deficient mirror neuron systems.[4]

I'd like to propose something else. What if the opposite were also possible? What if there are people who are actually born with overly functioning or highly sensitive mirror neuron systems? This may very well be the neurological origin of empaths and Highly Sensitive People as well as many other intuitive gifts.

Mirror-Touch Synesthesia

The discovery of mirror neurons also led another cognitive neuroscientist, Sarah-Jayne Blakemore, to discover a condition known as mirror-touch synesthesia. This is a condition that appears in hyper-empathetic people who can actually feel like they're being touched when they witness others being touched or feel pain when observing someone in pain. Sound at all similar to what we experience as empaths?

In a study conducted by researchers at the University College London, a group of mirror-touch synesthetes completed a questionnaire that was designed to measure empathy. The questionnaire was composed of true or false statements such as, "I can tune into how someone feels rapidly and intuitively." What they found was that the mirror-touch synesthetes scored significantly higher than normal people in their ability to experience empathy.[5]

Mirror-touch synesthesia could very well scientifically explain why physical empaths seem to "catch" or absorb the illnesses of other people, and also why empaths, as a whole, find violence absolutely unbearable to watch.

Morphogenetic Fields

To answer the important question of *how* we're able to absorb the emotional energy of others as empaths, we need to go back to the 1920's when the psychologist William McDougall wanted to find out how certain animals inherit abilities developed by their parents.[6]

McDougall created an experiment by putting baby rats into a tank of water from which they could escape up one of two ladders. One ladder had an electric current running through it, so the rats quickly learned to avoid that ladder and choose the other one.

Then McDougall tried the same experiment on the rat's children, and then on their children, and so on. What he discovered was that each generation learned more quickly than its parents. Thanks to this experiment, he proved that the inheritance of *acquired characteristics* is actually possible.

Wilfred Agar, a contemporary of McDougall from the University of Melbourne, decided to recreate this experiment, but he also tested the control group at the end of several generations. As you may or may not know, when a scientist performs an experiment, they always keep another identical group who are not subjected to the experiment. These are called the "control groups" and they work as a baseline of comparison. To his surprise and astonishment, the control group also showed the same ability to learn more quickly. But this was impossible because these rats had only been sitting passively in their cages! It appeared that these control rats had learned to avoid the electric ladder by some kind of telepathy.

However, it wasn't telepathy, according to cell biologist Rupert Sheldrake, but rather "morphic resonance," a theory he presented in his 1981 book *A New Science of Life*.[7] In this book, Sheldrake explained that the control group of rats "picked up" on the morphogenetic field of the trained rats in the same way that an iron bar can pick up the electrical field of a coil of wire and turn into a magnet. *It's basic induction.*

Sheldrake suggests that all species communicate with each other at a genetic and subconscious level through "morphogenetic fields" and "morphic resonance." He proposed that all living organisms, from cells to people, that belong to a certain group, tune in to the morphic field and through morphic resonance develop according to the programs within that field. Resonance only occurs between forms that are similar, so a monkey cannot take on the characteristics of a plant.

When an animal, let's say an eagle, learns a new skill that will benefit the survival of others, that skill is passed on through morphic resonance to all the other eagles of that species, and in doing so, allows that skill to be more easily learned by all the other eagles.

Essentially, what this means is that when we as humans learn to live more compassionately, we pass on these qualities to the rest of our species. On the other hand, when we develop fearful and neurotic habits, these are passed on to those around us too.

Therefore, according to science, our ability to internalize the emotions of others as empaths is actually the result of our ability to tune into the morphogenetic field that is composed of generation upon generation of human experience. In this way, our ancestors have actually helped to shape who we are and how we perceive the world.

Biocommunication

Biocommunication is a field of study that may explain how many of us empaths are able to feel the energy and emotions of other sentient beings, even those that don't have any mirror neurons or nervous systems such as plants, trees, certain animals, and places. The first time I heard about biocommunication was through a very unusual experiment conducted by Cleve Backster.

Backster was an operator of polygraph machines (or "lie detectors" as they are commonly called). But in February 1966, almost by accident, he came to discover what could be called "plant telepathy."

One day while he was in his office looking at his Dracaena cane plant, Backster wondered whether he could measure how long it would take for water to move up into the plant's leaves. He decided to attach the polygraphs electrodes to the plants leaves and water the pot. These electrodes measure the electrical conductivity of human skin, and he assumed they would also be able to register when the water reached the leaf.

What he didn't expect, was that the plant showed a surge in response to being watered, somewhat like you would measure when questioning a person. As Backster explained, "*So I began to wonder what I could do that would be a threat to the wellbeing of the plant, similar to the fact that a relevant question regarding a crime could be a threat to a person taking a polygraph test if they're lying.*"

His first idea to test the plants reactions was to dip a leaf into warm coffee. Nothing happened. He then decided to see what would happen if he used a flame to burn a leaf. The polygraph, he claimed, "*Went wild. The pen jumped right off the top of the chart.*" What is astonishing to note is that it was the *thought* of burning a leaf (he didn't have any matches in the room) to which the polygraph showed an immediate response!

Another interesting example was Backster's observation of the plant's polygraph reaction when he poured boiling water down the sink. Why would hot water going into the sink affect the plant with such a response? He theorized that the live microscopic organisms that accumulated in the drain were being killed by the hot water, hence the response from the plant. Somehow, the bacteria could emit signals that were received many feet away by another life form.

To test this theory out he dropped brine shrimp into boiling water and the plant appeared to register the shrimp's distress. It seemed impossible, but the plant was demonstrating some kind of sentient, even telepathic, awareness.

Encouraged by his findings, he continued experimenting further; wiring up yoghurt bacteria, eggs, and even human sperm to the polygraph. In 1990, Backster wrote his own book detailing all of his research with plants and human cells titled *Primary Perception.*[8]

This bit of history has a significant impact on our scientific understanding of what it means to be an empath. As sensitive people, we actually have the ability to respond to thought process through biocommunication. In fact, biocommunication may also explain why flora and fauna empaths can communicate with plant and animal species.

The Heart's Electromagnetic Field

One of the most interesting studies we can find to support the empath's ability to experience biocommunication and electromagnetic energy fields comes from the work of the HeartMath Institute.

The HeartMath Institute (HMI) has been carrying out research into the science of the heart for several decades now, and their findings present the notion that our heart plays a much more important role in the body than we first thought.

Until now, it has been generally thought by science that the heart is simply a pump of blood for the rest of our body and that our conscious awareness originates solely from our brains. But according to HMI, the heart is a far more complex system.

Rollin McCraty Ph.D who's the Director of Research of HMI, claims that after several scientific experiments, the results suggest that consciousness actually emerges from the brain and body acting together, and that the heart plays a particularly significant role in this process.[9]

HMI's research shows that the heart is a sensory organ that processes information separately from the brain and has a sophisticated nervous system which is referred to as the "heart brain." This actually enables the heart to learn, remember, and even make independent decisions. In a separate study, they concluded that the heart receives intuitive information faster than the brain, by a second or more, adding further evidence of the "heart brain" connection.[10]

What's more, the heart also communicates information to the brain and throughout the body via electromagnetic field interactions. For many years we've been able to measure the brain's magnetic fields using equipment like EEGs (electroencephalogram) and MEGs (Magnetoencephalography). But only through recent developments have we started paying attention to the "heart's field." What HMI found is that compared to the electromagnetic field produced by the brain, the heart's electrical field is about *60 times greater* in amplitude, and permeates every cell in the body. Not only that, but the magnetic component is approximately 5000 times stronger than the brain's magnetic field and can be detected several feet away from the body with Superconducting Quantum Interference Device (SQUID) based magnetometers.

In other words, the heart is a source of our consciousness: it creates its own electromagnetic field that carries emotional information outside of ourselves, and it is the receiver of bioelectromagnetic communication from within and outside the body. This explains why we can so easily tune into other people's energy as empaths. We can actually *feel* the energy emitted from other people's hearts.⌉

The deeper we delve into the research conducted by the HeartMath Institute, the more we can understand why we were born with the capacity to feel other's emotions and even illnesses as empaths.

For example, the researchers at HMI set out to determine whether the heart's electromagnetic field in one person could be detected and measured in another person when the pair were seated three feet away from each other. The results were positive.[11]

In another experiment, The Electricity of Touch, they asked the participants to hold hands in order to measure whether the heart's electromagnetic energy could be detected. They were able to successfully measure the transference of energy. In the paper, the author states that although additional research should be conducted, "when people touch or are in proximity, a transference of the electromagnetic energy produced by the heart occurs."[12]

The implications of this are significant. This discovery could be one of the first scientific studies to shed some light in how many alternative healing practices such as therapeutic touch, qigong, and reiki work, among others.

But how can we as empaths make use of this scientific evidence? What we should understand is that our hearts can actually *detect* the energy of those around us. This detection changes the electromagnetic field and blood pressure within our bodies so that every cell within us tunes into what others are experiencing.

If we are always giving and receiving electromagnetic signals, what does that mean for us as empaths when we feel the anger, fearfulness, depression, and other negative emotions of others? Can we influence those emotions with positive or more beneficial emotions of our own?

This study concludes that we can in fact transform at a cellular level other people's "negative" emotions into lighter ones by radiating empathy, care, compassion, and love from our own heart fields.

According to the research and studies that we've explored in this chapter, being an empath is not only scientifically valid, but it is also a stunningly complex and valuable gift to possess. Although our sensitivity means that we're more prone to experiencing pain and distress, we are also more receptive and compassionate, which ultimately makes life more rich and rewarding.

Chapter 7 – The Shamanic Understanding of Being an Empath

When I first moved to Australia, I spent a long time trying to readjust. After spending most of my childhood immersed in wild natural environments and surrounded by cultures that lived in deep harmony with everything that was living, it was strange to enter such a different society.

In shamanic cultures, the universe is seen as a living, interconnected web that is energetic and vibrational at its core and is constantly evolving. Shamanic people believe that there are no artificial boundaries in the world between that which is seen and that which is hidden; each level of consciousness is accessible.

But while this kind of total openness to existence is valuable to have when you're in a community of people who live in harmony of nature, such openness can quickly turn into a burden when you live in fast-paced suburbia.

Within weeks of moving to Australia I realized that I didn't want to feel so much anymore: it was frightening to walk by crowds of people and realize that so many of them carried waves of anger, bleak emptiness, resentment, and bitterness inside.

What surprised me the most was that the majority of these people were actually deaf and blind to their own emotions; they were completely numbed out. Not only could they not connect to their own feelings, but they lacked the ability to truly understand others.

It's unsurprising that so many empaths these days seek solitude as a form of protection against feeling emotionally depleted. Our environments are so hectic and constantly busy that allowing our senses to be completely open often results in a sensory overload. How can you tell where you begin and others end when there is so much frantic energy surrounding you?

The more I immersed myself in Australian city life, the more I began to wonder about my own energetic boundaries. I started to ponder questions such as, "What does my energetic boundary actually feel like?" "Which emotions are really mine?" and "How does the energy of the crowd influence me in other ways (e.g. physically, mentally, and socially)?"

As these questions crossed my mind, I started observing myself. What I noticed was an intricate connection between my breath and my boundaries. When I consciously breathed with intent, strongly and evenly, I found the center of my energy and sense of individuality. But when I breathed shallowly, the awareness of myself became weak and frail. In this way, the breath helped me to understand energy and energetic boundaries.

Energetic Wisdom

One of the ways our energetic boundaries can be illustrated is through the ancient Incan way of viewing the world. In Incan teachings, there is an understanding of the way the world works known in quechua (their ancient language) called "*Kawsay Pacha*," or living energy. To the shamanic Inca peoples, nature is alive and responsive, the cosmos is a vibrating field of pure energetic frequencies, and the world is as conscious of us and we are of it.

81

"*Kawsay Pacha*," living energy, or what some would call "Spirit," expresses itself in two fundamental types of energy: "Sami" and "Hucha." *Sami* is a lighter, more refined, and ordered energy that infuses the world with harmony and balance. *Hucha*, on the other hand, is the opposite; it's a heavy and disordered energy and it is only produced by human beings.

All of existence is constantly interchanging these energies in a reciprocal give and take relationship. This sacred reciprocity is known in quechua as "*Ayni.*"

You may think that *Hucha*, being a heavy energy, is something bad, dark or negative. It's not. Hucha is simply energy that we have received that is incompatible or disharmonious with our inner being and therefore becomes heavy for us to carry.

In the West, we easily reduce everything to dualities: things are either good or bad, right or wrong, correct or incorrect. But heaviness is a relative concept, which is why the Incan culture uses it to describe energy. Energy is neither good nor bad; it simply varies in vibrational density.

For example, if over time you accumulate "heavy" psychological energy that is imbalanced or disharmonious with your Soul, you will interpret this energy as anger, sadness or fear and begin to behave in self-destructive ways if you aren't aware of. The more heavy "Hucha" energy stays in your body, the more you are weighed down with issues such as low self-esteem, anxiety, and depression.

This energy accumulation is precisely why we need to bring more Sami (light) energy into our bodies. The more "light" energy we bring, the more we cleanse and let go of the heaviness inside of us, and the easier we'll find it to live in harmony with the world around us.

What I've found is that heavy Hucha energy is usually created by us humans because of our inability to live in reciprocity with each other. Unlike animals and the rest of life that flows perfectly with existence, we tend to resist and cut ourselves off due to our mental fears and desires. As empaths, we tend to either take on too much heavy energy from others, or alternatively, completely shut ourselves away. YUSSS.

The Incas, as well as many other wise shamanic traditions, understood very well the nature of energy exchange and those born with the gift of sensing it.

Ancient Healers and Visionaries

Traditional shamans and medicine women throughout history were not only healers; they were also visionaries, divination practitioners, mediums, dreamers, psychics, creators, and teachers of their communities.

But one thing all of these shamans, healers, and mystics had in common was that they were born with the gift of sensing and embodying energy. In other words, they were empaths.

As empaths, we are the modern day healers of our time. Because of our intense connection to all that is, our heightened sensitivity towards our internal and external worlds, as well as our deep desire to help others, it is our divine birthright to be healers, transformers, and co-creators of existence.

83

The shamanic Quechua word for empath is "*Qawaq*" which means "*one who sees*." It comes from the verb "*Qaway*" which means "*to see*" the living energy. The Incas believe that people born with the ability to experience the energy of others have a great blessing as they are able to connect to their Souls and the Spirit of existence much more easily than others.

The Incas describe the empath experience as happening when two living energies (for example, humans, animals, mountains) first meet and their energy bubbles touch each other, which is known as "*Tinkuy*." Once a person encounters another person's energy bubble, something we call "*Tupay*" starts to occur, where the two people begin to experience a collision of contrasts and differences between their energies, creating a confusion.

It's at this point that the empath who has learned to master their gift tries to distinguish the type of energy of the person, whether it is "*Yanantin*"; a completely opposing energy, or "*Masintin*"; an energy similar in frequency. That is when, in the Inca culture, you apply "*Taqe*," an attempt to harmonize these two living forces.

Although mastering these skills takes years of practice, what's important to remember is that energies we perceive as heavy or "evil" cannot do anything to us, unless we consciously or unconsciously agree to it.

This is why in shamanic teachings the accumulation and use of "personal power" is so important. Personal power is not about imposing or "dominating" another person; it is about being able to command our own energy.

By increasing our levels of Sami (light energy) throughout our daily lives, we raise our levels of consciousness and move toward our natural state of greater personal power. We'll explore how to introduce more of this light energy into our bodies as empaths later in this book.

For now, here's a shamanic mantra which will help you to ground yourself, purify your energy, and strengthen your energy field. This mantra invokes Pachamama, which is the Andean word for "mother earth." Chanting "pachamama" will help you introduce more Sami (light energy) into your body and release any hucha (heavy energy) within you.

Shamanic Pachamama Mantra

Find a quiet place outside in nature. Look for a place that has grass, dirt, rocks or sand – the more natural the better. Try to avoid standing on cement or bitumen as these are not as grounding because they have been processed and compacted. You may even like to take off your shoes if it isn't too cold or wet. Skin to earth contact is very powerful. However, if you prefer to leave your shoes on, that's fine too.

Once you have found a beautiful natural place, drop into your body and connect with your breath. Notice what it's like to stand or sit on top of the earth. Be mindful of the energy around you – what is it like to be in nature? Can you feel the buzz of life around you? Become very curious about how you feel when you stand in nature. What does the wind feel like on your face? What sounds and smells are your senses drinking in? Notice that everything your body is feeling and sensing is a manifestation of Mother Earth – Pachamama. As you stay rooted to the earth like a tree, allow yourself to be enchanted by the beauty of the Earth Mother. See her hair billow in the trees around you. Feel her breath as the soft wind against your neck. Hear her voice through the trill of crickets and chirping of birds. See her move through the birds drifting through the sky. As you become conscious and in tune with your surroundings, gain a sense of Pachamama's presence. Really feel her there with you. When you sense her energetic presence, you may like to hum, sing, or internally chant "Pachamama." Draw out the word and say it in whatever way feels the most right. For example, you might say over and over again "paaaaach-aaa-maaaaa-maaaaa." As you chant this shamanic mantra, feel your body opening and shedding off layers of dark energy. You may even like to visualize these layers of toxic energy falling onto the earth like raindrops or tree bark.

Continue this mantra for as long as you like. When you are finished, internally thank Pachamama for helping you to become grounded, strengthened, and energetically cleansed.

Chapter 8 – The Mystical Understanding of Being an Empath

"What is to give light must endure burning." – **Viktor E. Frankl**

What science has recently proven about the universe has already been known by mystics for millennia: that everything is fundamentally energy and we are all One. Science calls this interconnected web of energy "entanglement theory," but for thousands of years Buddhists have called this "*Dharmakaya*," Taoists have called it the "*Tao*" and Hindus have referred to this as "*Brahman*." Tao of Wu – RZA

Since the dawn of humanity, the mysterious and profound concept of Oneness has been written and spoken about extensively. Through the ages, countless yogis, spiritual masters, and enlightened beings such as Gautama Buddha, Jesus, Lao Tzu, Mahavira, Ramakrishna, and modern mystics such as Amma, Gangaji, Eckhart Tolle, and Sadhguru, among many others, have all spoken about Oneness.

The experience of Oneness has been called by many different names across many different cultures. It has been referred to as enlightenment, wholeness, illumination, love, moksha, satori, heaven, awakening, self-realization, among countless other names. Yet, all of these words have come to describe the same thing: that there is ultimately no energetic separation and we are all expression of the same Source.

Our oldest spiritual quest as human beings has been to perceive our own entanglement, to sense our own interconnectedness with all things and search for completion;

87

to finally find home. Deep down, we've always wanted to reunite and become "One" with the universe, to experience atonement (at-one-ment) with all that is. Yet as empaths, this very same feeling of connectedness we share with other living beings also tends to burden us. But why?

As empaths we come into this world with a highly developed ability to *feel* the Oneness around us. Because we are all metaphysically connected whether we want to be or not, tuning into this reality has become second nature to us. Yet this sensitivity and receptivity to the energetic Oneness all around us also means that we tend to quickly become enmeshed with other people. And when we are unable to differentiate ourselves and our feelings from others, serious problems start to arise.

Without being able to draw a line between "us" and "others," we end up experiencing problems such as codependency, self-esteem problems, abuse, and the tendency to take on everyone else's energetic "stuff." This is why it's so important for us to discover our individuality and establish boundaries: it's a sign of a mature and healthily functioning human being. Can you imagine how chaotic this world would be if none of us knew which feelings were ours, and which feelings were others'? Boundaries help us to experience clarity. As much as I love you, I do not wish to merge with you and take on your problems, and I'm sure you feel the same way too.

Life is a journey of growth and maturation on all levels, including the physical, mental, emotional, soul, and spiritual planes of existence. Picture a flower: it doesn't simply bloom into existence in an instant, instead, it goes through various stages of growth. The same applies to us as human beings. In order to find spiritual freedom (Oneness) and liberation from the illusion of separation and suffering, we must first master the basics and learn to love and take care of ourselves. This development of self-love requires us to create clear boundaries and a sense of distinct identity. Only once we can master the ability to separate ourselves from others and take care of our needs can we begin to truly help others, and ultimately to transcend the ego.

As an empath, you are the mystic of today's world. As a multi-sensory being, you are born with the refined ability to connect to the Soul essence of those around you. Yet due to your early life conditioning, these multi-sensory gifts have gone into overdrive, or else have been largely numbed out as a protection strategy. It is by learning how to balance your human experience with your spiritual experience that you will be able to experience what is known as freedom, or "Unio Mystica" (Mystical Union) with the Divine. Although being an empath may feel like a curse at times, its purpose is to both remind you of the Oneness of life, as well as provide you an opportunity to grow into the awakened being you're destined to become. It is our goal to help initiate you into this sacred journey of growth through this book. One of the most important practices we can use to grow deeply as empaths is known as Shadow Work. Shadow Work is about facing our inner darkness and immersing it in the light of conscious awareness and compassion. We'll explore this topic in the next chapter.

I feel like I finally understand.

89

Chapter 9 – The Dark Side of Being an Empath

As empaths, our lives aren't always full of love and light. Certainly, on the surface to other people, we appear warm, kindhearted, and caring. But deep beneath this facade we can also carry chasms of darkness, despair, and suppressed inner monsters.

One of the biggest struggles empaths have is acknowledging this inner darkness. Among the hundreds of empaths I've worked with, the vast majority have struggled to accept, and sometimes even acknowledge, the presence of the Shadow Self within them. This struggle is often followed by intense emotions such resistance, disbelief, denial, depression, anger, and fear.

According to Swiss psychiatrist Carl Jung, the Shadow Self is a place within the unconscious mind that is full of the thoughts, feelings, habits, desires, and impulses that we have rejected from ourselves. These parts were banished at different periods in our lives because they were deemed to be unacceptable, "bad," fearsome, "evil," disgusting," abhorrent, or somehow inadequate. Through time, these isolated parts formed the Shadow Self, or Dark Side within us that lurks in our subconscious minds. Therefore, most of us aren't aware of its presence.

But although we may doubt the existence of darkness within us, coming to understand and directly experience this darkness is the key to unlocking the process of healing both within ourselves, and eventually within others.

The Birth of the Shadow Self

Like most of our conditioning, our Shadow Selves began to develop in childhood. As children, the moment we began to separate the world into "good/bad," "nice/nasty," "right/wrong" was the moment that we learned how to divide ourselves. The more we divided ourselves, the more we rejected and repressed certain aspects of our personalities and characters, and thus, the bigger our Shadow Selves grew.

Our Shadow Selves are primarily the product of our conditioning. The conditioning we received as children, and continue to receive as adults, is composed of all the beliefs, ideals, values, superstitions, and moral codes of the people around us, including our families, friends, and societies. For example, we might have been taught that being happy was a "good" thing to feel, while feeling "angry" was a bad thing to feel. If we grew up in a family that punished us when we were angry, it's likely that we would have suppressed our anger in order to be "good" and not get punished.

Similarly, if we were raised in a religious environment, we might have been taught that sex is "dirty." Therefore, as teenagers we may have suppressed our sexual desire into the Shadow, and as adults we may struggle with problems like guilt, shame, sex addiction, infertility or even abusive relationships.

Not only were our Shadows formed from our conditioning, but they were also forged by our parents', family's, and society's collective Shadows, which in turn influenced our conditioning. In a sense, you could say that the people and environment around us unintentionally "infected" us with generation upon generation of residual suffering. Residual suffering is the leftover pain that we experience from issues that have gone before us such as wars, slavery, genocide, inequality, rape, abuse, murder, and betrayal. *I've heard of this*

In some way, shape or form, what has happened in the past has impacted us on various levels. Whether emotionally, physically, psychologically or spiritually, we all carry wounds not only from childhood, but also from our ancestors. Our mission as empaths is to decipher what that pain is, embrace it, and put it to rest. *I'm always doing this*

What is Locked Within the Shadow?

In order to heal our pain as empaths, it's vital that we take an honest look at our Shadow Selves. But before we do that, we have to know what to look for. Think of this process as taking a flashlight and exploring the damp caves of your innermost self. You can't know what you're supposed to look for without some light!

As mentioned previously, our Shadow Selves contain everything we judge as being unacceptable, bad, fearsome, evil, disgusting, abhorrent or somehow inadequate within us. Those who undertake Shadow Work are often shocked by what they find. But there's no need to fear. Your Shadow isn't out to hurt you, it simply wants you to acknowledge it and embrace it so it can find the light again.

There could be any number of things locked in the Shadow. In order to find, understand, and accept them, you have to be in a centered place. You can't approach exploring your Shadow from a place of self-hatred or judgment; otherwise you'll exacerbate your wounds. So if you don't feel prepared at this

92

time in your life to explore your Shadow, that's OK. You can simply read this section and keep it in mind for a later time.

Some of the most common emotions, desires, thoughts, and traits that are outlawed to the Shadow Self include:

- "Negative" emotions such as anger, hatred, jealousy, lust, greed, guilt, shame, envy, and despair
- Thoughts of a psychologically violent, manipulative, or graphic nature (e.g. abuse, suicide, torture, blackmail, etc.)
- Socially deviant desires such as thievery, fraud, murder, embezzlement, selling drugs, cannibalism, etc.
- Sexually deviant desires such as cheating on your partner, watching pornography, rape, pedophilia, sadism, necrophilia, bestiality, incest, bizarre fetishes, homosexuality/lesbianism (in some cultures), etc.
- Parental or culturally deviant traits such as being talkative, free-thinking, sensitive, emotional, expressive, flatulating in public, etc. ?

(Seriously?)

Virtually *anything* judged as inappropriate, weird or bad within ourselves is shut in the Shadow Self. And yes, some of this stuff is extreme! But not all of it is graphic. It is impossible to describe everything that could possibly be locked within the Shadow, so it's ultimately up to each one of us to discover what we have hidden away.

One thing you may not know is that our Shadows often possess many of our hidden *positive* qualities as well. These positive qualities include:

- Repressed and disowned gifts, e.g. empathy, wisdom, artistic capacities, ability to communicate with spirits, etc.
- Rejected personality traits such as kindness, compassion, ambition, independence, humor, passion, etc.

These positive qualities are what Robert Johnson in his book *Owning Your Own Shadow* refers to as "the gold within the Shadow." So your Shadow Self isn't only full of doom and gloom! There are many diamonds, pearls, and emeralds hidden in it as well.

Empaths and the Shadow Self

In order to heal ourselves, function well in the world, and reclaim our life purpose as empaths, it is vital that we learn how to identify and embrace our Shadow Selves. When we are not conscious of our Shadows, they have the tendency to secretly run our lives and sabotage our efforts to be happy.

Have you ever wondered why you have a habit of repeating the same relationship patterns and attracting the same types of toxic people over and over again? Have you ever wondered why you struggle on a daily basis with feelings of fatigue, anxiety, depression, and the inability to "cope" with life? Have you ever grappled with anger, guilt, and intense recurring fears? If so, this is your Shadow Self rearing its head.

Your Shadow is a dark omen, a powerful teacher that reveals to you the places in your life where you are energetically blocked. When you continue to ignore these signs, you perpetuate the cycle of your suffering. It's easy to point the finger at other people and blame their disturbing energy for our pain, but this doesn't solve our problems. It's ultimately up to us, as empaths, to take responsibility for our happiness and explore what is happening within *us* that is causing us to suffer.

That's what I'm trying to do

As a student of life and spiritual mentor, I deal with the Shadow Self on almost a daily basis. Through the years, it has become clear that empaths struggle with a number of shadow issues which manifest as a variety of physical, emotional and mental disorders.

The deeper I've dug within both myself and other empaths, the more I've discovered that the root of our pain comes from both suppressing and repressing our sensitivity, and also attaching to and identifying with pain. *That's exactly my problem*

Here are some of the most common Shadow issues and symptoms that we face as empaths:

Physical disorders

- Addictions, e.g. to sugar, caffeine, food, alcohol, smoking, drugs, sex, adrenaline
- Binge-eating or under-eating, i.e. eating a lot in one go, or depriving yourself of food
- Avoidance of certain people or situations
- Chronic unexplained fatigue
- Fibromyalgia (chronic aching muscles)
- Headaches and migraines
- Constant colds and flu
- High blood pressure
- Dizziness
- Shaking
- Knots in stomach/butterflies

95

- Desire to scream
- Digestive problems
- Oversleeping or insomnia

Emotional Disorders

- Adopting the role of the care-taking martyr
- Exaggerated emotional reactions to the losses or traumas of acquaintances, strangers, fictional characters, or animals
- Inability to express emotional vulnerability
- Repressed anger
- Constant unhappiness/depression
- Feeling overwhelmed all the time by anxiety

Mental Disorders

- Neurosis or obsessive compulsive behaviors
- Negative self-talk
- Blaming
- Criticizing others
- Deeply ingrained cognitive distortions
- Weariness
- Confusion
- Inability to concentrate
- Mental fog
- Hypervigilance *sensory sensitivity/exaggerated intensity of behaviors whose purpose is to detect activity*

You might like to review this list again and see how many of these shadow issues you can identify with. Take your time, and pay attention to which signs catch your eye.

Among all these issues, a few stand out as the major problems most empaths struggle with. But before I elaborate on these

cognitive - the mental action or process of acquiring knowledge & understanding through thought experience & senses

issues, I want you to know that facing your Shadows can be confronting as it can often feel like your self-image is falling apart. After all, most of us innocently believe that we are one hundred percent kind and loving people. Anything that challenges this self-image of ours can be disturbing.

While it is true that we are warm, kind, and loving people, we also need to get real here. We need to be honest with ourselves and have the courage to face ourselves with objectivity. We are not perfect, nor will we ever be. But that's OK. Life is a process of growth and learning, and one of the best possible ways you can grow is by facing your own Shadow.

Here are the dominant shadow issues the majority of empaths need to pay attention to:

1. Blame

Blame is one of the biggest issues that we face as empaths. When we attribute our suffering to others, we're essentially avoiding self-responsibility for our happiness. Certainly, we can feel the energy of others as our own, and this causes us suffering. But it is ultimately our choice to cling to this energy or not. Yes, the people around us can be insensitive, narcissistic, toxic, and sometimes even abusive, but it is up to us to take that energy on or let it flow through us. No one is responsible for taking away our happiness but us.

2. Projection

Projection is the psychological term for attributing our own psychological and emotional qualities to others. For example, we might look at another person and think they're judgmental, when in fact, we're projecting *our* judgmentalism onto them.

Because we're so confused about the energy we give and receive as empaths, it's very easy for us to project our own qualities onto other people. For example, it's common for empaths to project their emotional instability onto others, and believe that it is *other people* who are making them feel uncomfortable. If you think this might be a problem for you, we'll explore how to create stronger identity boundaries later in this book.

3. Introjection

Surprisingly, not many people know about introjection. Introjection is actually the opposite of projection, and it involves taking the feelings and attribute of another person, and unconsciously believing they are our own. For example, we might believe that we're depressive, when in fact, we've taken that attribute from someone we live with and have believed that it's our own.

Once again, this shadow quality is related to our confusion as empaths and our inability to distinguish what energy is ours, and what energy comes from other people. Introjection can be particularly dangerous because it causes us to carry around a large number of mistaken beliefs about ourselves. These mistaken beliefs often result in a lot of unnecessary heavy emotional baggage. We'll explore how to deal with introjection later in this book.

4. Victimization and Self-Pity

Self-victimization and self-pity are shadow twins that go hand-in-hand. When we feel excessively sorry for ourselves, we have the tendency to believe that we are victims of life or other people. The more we identify with the victim role, the more we filter life through this narrowed mental lens, and the more we attract situations into our lives that make us feel sorry for ourselves. Do you see how this is a vicious cycle? Our thoughts influence our reality, so when we believe that we're "at the mercy" of everyone else's energy, we start to behave in a way that reinforces this belief. In other words, we become self-fulfilling prophecies.

Because of the nature of our gifts, it can be very easy for us to fall into the victim trap. In fact, almost every empath at some point or another has identified with this role that takes away personal empowerment.

5. Martyrdom

The Martyr is another shadow role that we have a tendency of slipping into unconsciously. While similar to the victim role, the Martyr role is a bit more complex. On one side, Martyrs are kind, generous, supportive, and selfless. But underneath, a Martyr is full of fear, paranoia, and low self-worth.

In my line of work, I've seen the Martyr role frequently being played out by empaths, often without them even knowing it. As we tend to absorb the pain of others, many of us start believing that it is our "mission" to suffer so that others can be healed. Pretty soon, "righteous suffering" becomes a source of self-worth for many empaths. But here's the thing: Martyrdom not only harms us, but it also indirectly harms other people.

Empaths who have adopted the role of Martyrs tend to take on the following attributes:

- They have a hard time saying "no" and setting personal boundaries
- They stay in abusive friendships or relationships with the hope that they can "fix" the person they're with, even despite ailing health
- They blame the selfishness of humanity for their emotional suffering
- They frequently seek to reassure themselves of their innocence
- They exaggerate their level of suffering, hardship or mistreatment
- They refuse to take responsibility for decisions that have caused them suffering
- They portray themselves as the righteous, self-sacrificing, "nice guy/girl," saint, caretaker or hero
- They coerce others into doing what they want by portraying themselves as the noble sufferer
- They actively seek recognition by creating drama

These attributes might sound harsh, but we have all experienced them to some extent. Most importantly, as empaths we are almost always completely unaware that we're playing this role.

6. Avoidance and Addiction

Because the emotional and sometimes physical pain we experience on a daily basis frequently becomes too intense, we tend to avoid it at all costs. Empaths tend to avoid pain and even other people in a variety of ways: through food, work, shopping, internet, drugs, alcohol, and other forms of numbing addiction. Because of the intensity of our sensitivity, addiction is the easiest way to soothe our pain because it distracts us from the reality we're trying to avoid.

7. Codependency

As deeply sensitive and caring people by nature, we have a tendency to be problem solvers who love to help others. Because we can feel the pain of others so acutely, it seems almost cruel for us *not* to help when we're aware of how much pain the people around us are going through. Unfortunately, when this intense desire to help others is coupled with self-esteem issues and childhood trauma, it's a recipe for codependency.

Codependency is the tendency to excessively rely on our relationships for our emotional and psychological fulfillment. In other words, without a certain relationship in our lives, we feel like we are "nothing" and we find it impossible to be alone with ourselves. Codependency is essentially relationship addiction. In codependent relationships, it is common for one partner to be the enabler (usually the empath) and the other to be the abuser. Abuse can either be directed towards the enabler in physical, emotional or verbal form, or abuse can be directed towards addictions to drugs, alcohol, gambling, etc.

Empaths that have a tendency to fall into codependent and enabling roles tend to totally sacrifice their needs for the abusive partner, and keep quiet about their partner's abuse. This relationship dynamic is often seen to evolve between the empaths and narcissists, who have a tendency of attracting each other. (We'll explore empaths and narcissists in the next chapter.) Obviously, codependency is a serious problem that perpetuates the cycle of pain within empaths.

8. Low self-worth

Underlying almost every issue that empaths face is low self-worth. Our low self-worth is responsible for our tendency to give away our power, put ourselves in minimizing or manipulative roles, and lose ourselves in addictions.

Although on the surface it would appear that other people and their energy is the main source of our problems, deep down we know that it's not. It is our inability to take care of ourselves and empower ourselves that causes us to suffer. It is our identification with the stories in our heads that create our endless cycles of pain and inability to process other people's energy.

Low self-worth is always underpinned by a range of core beliefs. Core beliefs are the main beliefs we developed throughout life that were influenced by our parents, families, teachers, friends, and societies.

Common core beliefs that we carry include:

- I am not worthy of love.
- I am bad.
- I am a failure.
- I don't deserve to be happy.
- I deserve to be punished.
- I am weak.
- I am all alone.

Once we learn how to uncover our core beliefs, we can start to unravel the knot of blocked energy within us.

9. Repression

When the emotional torrents of energy around us begin to flood our nervous systems, it is common for us as empaths to shut down. Whether consciously or unconsciously, almost all empaths have repressed the toxic energy absorbed from others as a defense mechanism. These repressed, or locked away, emotions end up dwelling in our Shadow Selves and become trapped as chronic illness in our bodies.

The reason why we repress certain types of emotions both from others and also from ourselves is because we usually have no idea how to handle such emotions. Not only that, but our conditioning as children taught us that expressing certain emotions such as anger were "wrong" and deserved to be punished. What message did that leave us with? Thanks to our conditioning and lack of emotional tools, the only option we have is to shut away these feelings out of complete fear. When feelings such as despair, insecurity, anxiety, rage, lust, and self-loathing are locked away, we almost immediately "forget about them" because we have essentially thrown away the key. Through time, the more we repress, the more energetic blocks we build within our body-mind organism, and the more psychological and physical dis-ease we develop. Not only that, but these emotions are pushed deeper and deeper within ourselves, making them increasingly harder to vent.

Although these shadow issues might be disheartening, please don't let your heart get heavy. The best thing about revealing the inner Shadow is that we can finally become conscious of destructive and sabotaging patterns of behavior within us. In other words, we're able to shine the light of consciousness into our dark inner caverns, and make friends with our monsters. And when we're conscious and willing to work through these issues, we're finally able to heal. By reading this chapter, you're already on the way to a massive shift in your life.

We'll explore how you as an empath can bring about deep, life-changing healing to your Shadow Self in the rest of this book. But first, let's explore a topic every empath needs to familiarize themselves with: the empath-narcissist connection.

Chapter 10 – Empaths and Narcissists

One of the most important lessons we can ever learn as highly sensitive and intuitive empaths is safeguarding and preserving our energy. When life force energy is flowing through us unhindered, we feel light, spacious, calm, compassionate, grounded, and full of vivacious energy. But when the life force energy in us becomes blocked or preyed on by others, we feel depleted, depressed, anxious, confused, irritable, and exhausted.

The field of psychosomatic medicine has shown that our energy levels directly influence our perception of life. In other words, when we're energetically depleted, we're more prone to suffering from chronic mental and emotional illnesses. However, when we're energetically enlivened, we're more prone to experiencing emotions such as joy, love, and gratitude. There's a reason why energetic people are perceived as being happy-go-lucky, and depressed people are perceived as being "low-energy" types – and that is the psychosomatic connection between the mind and the body, or energy and emotions.

As empaths, we need to be extremely vigilant about the energy we permit into our lives. We need to learn how to create balance between what we give and what we receive because energy is such a precious gift. Without energy, how can we feel happiness and a sense of well-being? Without energy, how can we nurture ourselves and those we love? Without energy, how can we live lives of true meaning, purpose, and significance?

Like many things in life, we often take energy for granted, not really understanding or appreciating its value. We are so used to giving away our energy to others, that we forget to keep any for ourselves. Therefore, it's often only when we *lose* our energy that we start appreciating its profound role in our lives.

Two of the most dangerous and energetically abusive relationships we tend to get sucked into as empaths are with narcissists and energy vampires. When it comes to energy preservation, narcissists and energy vampires are the two types of people that deplete our energy the most. In this chapter, we'll explore the irresistible attraction, toxic dynamics, and potential solutions for the empath-narcissist connection, and in the next chapter we'll explore the empath and energy vampire connection.

Empaths and Narcissists

"I had a narcissist in my life that hooked me by inundating me with adoration. I didn't understand why others didn't think this person was as great as I was seeing them ... until I had served my purpose, or became boring to them, and their true colors started showing. After feeling closeness for some time, I was suddenly hit with constant insults and beratement." – Anonymous empath reader from lonerwolf.com

By nature, we are gentle and perceptive. We can see the hidden fears behind smiles, the tension behind smooth and polished personalities, the anger underneath goodwill, and the hurt right before people lash out. Fundamentally, we are multisensory beings who see "beyond the veil" of people's personas, and feel other's innermost emotions as our own.

106

A narcissist, on the other hand, is the exact opposite of an empath. Emotionally, narcissists are like brick walls who see and hear others, but fail to understand or relate to them. As a result of their emotional shallowness, narcissists are essentially devoid of all empathy or compassion for other people. Lacking empathy, a narcissist is a very destructive and dangerous person to be around, particularly when they overlap with more extreme sociopathic traits.

The emotional blindness of narcissists can be particularly dangerous because it means that they will stop at nothing to please themselves. Because they're unable to feel anything towards other people, they will use, manipulate, lie to, shame, bully, and abuse others without remorse. Therefore, to an emotionally blind person, life becomes solely centered around the self and the creation of a lavish, desirable, and powerful ego. Other people merely become obstacles to be destroyed or stepping stones towards creating this idealized identity.

The Birth of Narcissism

In order to help us understand our connection with narcissists, it's beneficial for us to firstly understand *why* and *how* narcissists came to be the way they are. Understanding why and how narcissists came to develop their emotional blindness will help us to show discerning compassion instead of anger and resentment towards them (which further depletes our energy). After all, associating with a narcissist is one of the most disturbing, frightening, and upsetting experiences we can have in life.

So the question is, are narcissists born or made? Almost all behavioral psychologists have observed that narcissism is actually a trait that is taught or programmed into certain children at a young age. Narcissism seems to stem from traumatic childhood experiences, such as physical or emotional abandonment and poverty or abuse, but also by parental priming. For example, parents can prepare their children to develop narcissistic personalities through promoting ideas that they are more special or entitled than other children. Slowly, such children internalize these beliefs, truly believing that they're better than others, which stunts their capacity to develop empathy.

On the other hand, narcissists that experienced traumatic childhoods tend to overcompensate and disguise their feeling of inner worthlessness by creating and hiding behind idealized versions of themselves. Any time this idealized image is threatened, the narcissist will lash out in blatant or passive ways to ensure that their self-image is maintained.

Depending on the narcissist's childhood conditioning and genetic predispositions, they will fall into a number of different "types" of narcissistic behavior.

There are actually two main types of narcissism, and four subtypes. The two main types of narcissists are known as the vulnerable and invulnerable narcissists, which I'll break down below:

Vulnerable Narcissists (VNs)

A vulnerable narcissist is generally a very emotionally (not empathetically) sensitive person who tends to be quiet or shy by nature. Yet to disguise their chronic feelings of self-hatred and unworthiness, VNs overcompensate by putting on a grandiose mask, seeking to merge their identities with other idealized versions. VNs have an unshakeable need to feel special about themselves and have little genuine regard for the feelings of others. VNs are primarily motivated by fear of rejection and abandonment. Thus they don't have the capacity to authentically love and care for others. Additionally, VNs use emotional manipulation (such as shaming, guilt-tripping and gaslighting) to secure sympathy and attention from others. Their lives are fueled by inferiority complexes which often stem from childhood mistreatment.

Invulnerable Narcissists (INs)

IN's reflect the stereotypical image of narcissists: highly self-confident people who are emotionally cold and ruthless. INs, unlike VNs, are thick-skinned and shamelessly seek for power, glory, recognition, and pleasure. INs often suffer from god complexes, believing themselves to be far superior to everyone else – and they have a pathological need to make that known.

Both types share similar traits such as using others to fuel their narcissistic delusions, blaming and criticizing, lack of empathy, unfaithfulness, and the need for power.

Both vulnerable and invulnerable narcissists can actually be broken down even further to four subtypes:

Amorous Narcissists

Amorous Narcissists measure their self-worth and grandiosity by how many sexual conquests they have under their belt. This type of person is known for using his/her charm to ensnare others with flattery and gifts, but then quickly disposing of their "conquests" once they become boring or don't meet the narcissist's needs. Amorous Narcissists are the ultimate relationship con artists, "gold diggers," and heart-breakers. At first glance they appear highly attractive, alluring, and amiable, but underneath they are only out to please and satiate their own needs and desires.

Compensatory Narcissists

Driven to compensate for past traumas, Compensatory Narcissists love creating larger-than-life illusions about themselves and their achievements. In order to regain power and control over their lives, this type of narcissist usually hunts out emotionally vulnerable people who will serve as the audience to their fabricated stage acts. In reality, this type of narcissist is extremely sensitive to criticism and will frequently look out for negative self-directed cues from others. Emotional abuse and manipulation are common methods of control used by this type.

Elitist Narcissists

This breed of person does anything to climb to the "top," win, and completely dominate others. Elitist Narcissists are convinced that they are better than everyone else, often due to their achievements or backgrounds (or simply the fact that they were raised that way). Thus they believe they deserve "special treatment." Their sense of entitlement bleeds into every area of life, from work to the family environment. Harboring a severely inflated self-image, Elitist Narcissists are skilled self-promoters, braggers, and one-uppers. They have a cutthroat need to be the best and to prove themselves to be intellectually superior all the time and at all costs.

Malignant Narcissists

The behavior of Malignant Narcissists often overlaps with that of antisocial or psychopathic personality disorders. Malignant Narcissists often have no regard or interest in moral vs. immoral behavior, and don't feel remorse for their actions. This subgroup is characterized by an arrogant and inflated sense of self-worth that delights in outsmarting others. This type of narcissist can often be found in prisons, gangs, and drug rehabilitation centers, although many manage to avoid the law.

As you can see, there are a number of different "flavors" of narcissism. Fortunately, by reading this list, you've now given yourself the power to pay attention to any red flags that pop up in the future. Knowledge is power.

But although being able to define and identify narcissists is useful, it isn't enough in and of itself. We also have to understand WHY we tend to get wound up in narcissistic relationships in the first place, and how to prevent this from reoccurring.

The Irresistible Empath-Narcissist Connection

At first glance, empaths and narcissists appear to have nothing in common at all. So why are we irresistibly drawn to them? While we feel *too* much, they don't feel anything at *all* towards others. While we are caring, they are callous and indifferent to anyone else but themselves. While we're focused on helping others, they are focused on worshiping and aggrandizing their ego.

Yet despite these opposing traits, we are nevertheless lured into the narcissist's circle like a moth is to a flame. Why do we repetitively fall into such a bizarre and damaging relationship with these types of people?

One of the major reasons that empaths and narcissists are attracted to each other is because of the empaths desire to help the narcissist, and the narcissist's desire to take advantage of the empath's emotional support. As I mentioned before, pity is our Achilles' Heel, and we often mistake it for the experience of love. Being highly perceptive of ways to exploit others, a narcissist will almost instantly pick up on this vulnerability, and will slowly manipulate us into playing their pity party game. This game is designed to both gain special attention, and also a loyal supporter or "groupie." The moment we're hooked, the narcissist will feed off our goodwill like an emotional parasite. But the truth is, underneath this charade there often *is* deep self-hatred and inner pain, which empaths can immediately feel, making it easier for us to buy into their charade. Being blinded by our desire to help the narcissist, we fall into his or her trap.

Another reason why we tend to fall into the disturbing gravitational pull of narcissists is because of their charming, but confusing, allure. Have you ever met a person who showers others with praise and is highly intelligent and charismatic ... yet there is something looming behind the surface which you can't quite pick up on? This person was most likely a narcissist. Later, you might discover conflicting messages as you spot a darker, more vicious side emerge in this person. Thus, you start becoming curious about this person in an effort to "figure them out." But, being masters of deception, they will eventually catch you in the web of their lies and manipulation.

The final, more spiritual explanation of why we tend to enter narcissistic relationships is because in meeting a narcissist, we meet our inverted or "reverse" selves. Because the fundamental laws of the universe are about creating balance and harmony, the same applies to our connection with narcissists. When we meet and fall into the gravitational pull of a narcissist, we are entering a significant life lesson that involves learning how to create boundaries, self-respect, and resilience. Through trial and error (and a lot of pain), our connection with narcissists teaches us the necessary lessons we need to become mature empaths. A narcissist, on the other hand, may experience great disturbance and disruption when an empath in their life leaves out of disgust, particularly one who is in a close relationship with them. Sometimes (but very rarely), this is enough for them to seek professional help, diagnosis, and assistance.

Once we've been brainwashed into believing that it's our place to "change," "fix," "heal," "support" or "cure" the narcissist in our lives, we quickly become emotionally enmeshed.

Poor Boundaries and Enmeshment

Both empaths and narcissists, from the very start, have poor boundaries. A narcissist will be willing to cross any boundary there is in order to uphold their inflated sense of self, and an empath doesn't really know what boundaries are due to their tendency to feel everything from everyone all the time. Therefore, both empaths and narcissists become enmeshed very rapidly because of their poorly established boundaries.

Thanks to this emotional entanglement, it's very easy for empaths to quickly lose touch with reality. It doesn't help that narcissists tend to play sickening mind games with the intent of keeping us docile, vulnerable, and subservient. As a result of our poor boundaries and sense of self, we begin to doubt ourselves. We're told that we're "selfish" for taking time out for ourselves, we're made to feel like terrible human beings for critiquing something, and we're told that we're being "too sensitive" and we're not remembering the details properly when in conversations with them.

One of the most popular ways narcissists control empaths is through emotional abuse, which is what creates the codependent/abuser connection often seen in empath-narcissist relationships. Because empaths can see the world through their partner's point of view, they frequently tend to completely mesh with the viewpoints of their abusers. So when an empath is told that he or she is uncaring from a narcissistic partner, the empath will genuinely feel as though they are a horrible person due to the fact that they can feel and embody the emotions of their partners. In other words, an empath's already fragile sense of self will become even weaker when they feel like horrible people around their narcissist partners. And if that empath's self-worth is already low to begin with, he or she will quickly start believing that he/she is a terrible person. In turn, this feeling of "not being enough" will fuel the empath's desire to prove themselves as a caring and loving person to their narcissistic partner – which is exactly what the narcissist wants. The more the narcissist causes the empath to doubt his/her goodness, the more the empath will seek validation, and the more control the narcissist will have. This vicious cycle quickly spirals into a toxic codependent connection in which the empath is dependent on the narcissist for his or her self-worth and identity.

Signs You Might Be in a Narcissistic Relationship

If you've reached this point in the book and the narcissist-empath connection sounds scarily familiar to you, the following signs may help you to gain clarity. See how many of these telltale narcissistic relationship signs you can identify with:

- He/she was extremely likeable and charming when you first met.
- It took you a while to discover his/her darker traits (e.g. once you were married).
- He/she is always talking about themselves, and every conversation will go back to their problems, desires, and opinions.
- He/she is obsessed with his/her physical appearance and will display signs of extreme vanity, e.g. only buying designer clothing, watches, expensive cosmetics.
- You must plan your life around his/her needs and wants.
- He/she takes a lot from you, but never gives back anything in return.
- He/she takes everything personally and will erupt into extreme anger when critiqued.
- He/she shows no signs of empathy or sensitivity towards other people's emotions.
- He/she is convinced they're superior to everyone in intellect, breeding, and basic human worth.
- He/she will enjoy belittling and defaming others if it makes him/her look good.
- He/she refuses to take responsibility for anything he/she did wrong – YOU will always be "responsible."
- He/she will emotionally manipulate you into feeling bad about yourself and will frequently play the victim.

115

- He/she will frequently gaslight you (gaslighting is a manipulation technique that makes you doubt your own sanity).
- He/she will want to have total control over you, e.g. he/she will want to know where you go, what you do, who you talk to, what you buy, etc.
- He/she will try to isolate you and make you distrust other people (so he/she has more control over you).
- He/she is emotionally unpredictable and you'll often be shocked by the level of rage and punishment they show towards you for no apparent reason.
- He/she is always, unequivocally, "right" about everything.

Take a few moments to reflect on this list and even re-read it if you feel like you might be trapped in a narcissistic relationship. Remember, narcissistic relationships aren't always romantic: they can often be experienced with our parents, siblings, and even friends.

Shattering Empath-Narcissist Codependency

Once an empath is stuck in the clutches of a narcissistic and codependent relationship, it can be difficult to get untangled. Because of the depletion of energy within the empath, finding the willpower to take a step back, look at the big picture, and cut off the connection can be extremely difficult.

Fortunately, shattering such a destructive connection is possible. If you're currently in, or have been in, a narcissistic relationship, and wish to exit or prevent such an affiliation from happening again, there are a number of healing paths you can follow. Here are a few:

1. Take a vacation.

If you're able to, create as much physical distance as you can between you and your narcissistic partner. For example, you could take a simple family vacation by visiting a relative, or actually take a holiday. Physical distance will help you to remove the narcissist's energy from your life so you can begin to think and feel clearly again. You'll benefit from limiting contact from the narcissist as much as possible, e.g. not answering your phone, texting, or emailing your partner. Try limiting your contact for a week, and reflect on how you feel. The narcissist will likely be infuriated, so that's something you'll need to be prepared to deal with in whatever way you can.

Once you're sure that your relationship is toxic, you can make the leap and practice no contact. No contact involves leaving the narcissist and cutting off all sources of contact, i.e. phone calls, emails, text messages, visits, or social media interaction.

2. Explore who you are.

One of the major issues empaths struggle with is a weak sense of self, and therefore poor boundaries. Self-discovery is one of the best ways to understand who you are and to create stronger boundaries. Try taking personality tests (both of us have published numerous free tests on our website), reading self-exploratory books, and delving into materials that will help you understand yourself better. This book is a great start!

3. Practice self-love and self-care.

Refuse to dedicate all of your time to others. Regularly set aside time for yourself and things you enjoy doing. The more you take care of yourself, the more of your energy will return, and the more confidence you will gain in cutting ties with the narcissist in your life. Take care of your body, your emotions, your energy, and your dreams. Explore books and workshops that can help you learn to practice self-love better.

4. Try the gray rock method.

One of the best ways to escape predatory relationships such as those with narcissists is by practicing what is known as the "gray rock" method. The gray rock method is essentially a way of making yourself so boring to a narcissist that they will eventually leave you alone. Narcissists thrive on drama and reaction. When you deprive them of that, they quickly start to lose interest in you.

For example, if the narcissist blames you for everything bad that is happening to them, nod, and make them believe that you're taking all the blame. When they try to push your buttons, don't react, simply sit there mundanely. Do not talk about anything remotely interesting with them, and when they talk to you, simply respond with bland answers and agree.

While this method can be difficult, it can be mastered after practice and commitment.

5. Develop a support network.

Speak with trusted friends and family members about how you're feeling. If you don't have anyone you trust, contact a support network online or via the phone. Sometimes getting the perspective of another person is all you need to get up and leave.

There are many other ways to prevent narcissistic entanglement, but these five points are found to be useful by many empaths. We'll explore other empowering methods of self-love and support in chapter 16.

Narcissists Who Disguise as Empaths

One of the strangest disguises that some narcissists take is that of being empaths. "How is it possible for a narcissist to disguise as an empath?" you might wonder. But yes, surprisingly, it is possible, particularly in the spiritual community.

Take Lauren for example. Lauren is a 47 year old caretaker who is best friends with her childhood friend Cecilia. Cecilia constantly claims that she can "feel" other people, yet Lauren has always felt that Cecilia could never really feel her in any deep way. In conversations, Cecilia constantly tells Lauren what she "feels" about other people, and frequently directs all the attention back to herself. When Lauren disagrees with Cecilia, Cecilia essentially tells her "no, I'm right, I can feel their energy," which translates to, "shut up, conversation over." Throughout the years, Lauren observes that what Cecilia thinks is "feeling" people is actually judgmental criticism, jealousy or projecting her own insecurities onto others. When Cecilia discovers the term "empath" she suddenly declares that she's an empath. When Lauren tells Cecilia that she thinks that she might be an empath as well, Cecilia says in a condescending tone, "No ... I don't *feel* that about you. Empaths just *know* these things and I can sense that you definitely *aren't* one." Lauren relates that she loves Cecilia, but she feels drained around her, intensely frustrated, constantly devalued, and completely disregarded.

119

As we can see, the term "empath" can actually be misused. A narcissist or emotionally unaware person can easily use this term to build an idealized version of themselves. Not only that, but identifying as an empath can support these people's belief in their "unequivocal rightness" and everyone else's perceptual "wrongness" because they can "feel things" other people can't.

We have to be mindful when we're seeking guidance from mentors and healers that these people aren't actually narcissists disguised as empaths. Furthermore, we have to be careful that *we* don't use our gifts as a way to undervalue other people who may not be as emotionally receptive or perceptive as us.

Chapter 11 – Empaths and Energy Vampires

You have that feeling again inside: it's the feeling of intense lethargy, the kind of lethargy that makes you feel like your veins have been bled dry. As you try to focus on what the person in front of you says, a dull throb emerges in the back of your skull, and you wince as the pain creeps through your head. The more you interact with this person, the more blurry your periphery becomes, and the more exhausted and mentally "spacey" you feel. But it gets worse – when you try to end the conversation, you feel as though you're being energetically dragged into continuing talking. There doesn't seem to be any way of escaping.

Have you experienced this before? What I am describing here is a common scenario faced by many empaths all over the world, all the time. This feeling of intense fatigue is experienced when an empath comes in contact with what is known as an *energy vampire*.

An energy vampire is quite simply a person who feeds off your emotional or psychic energy. If you've ever met an energy vampire (and you probably have), you'll get the distinct feeling that this person has an intense need to prey off the vitality of others. There is a kind of acute neediness present in energy vampires which can be quite overwhelming and depleting to those they come in contact with.

An energy vampire could be anyone: a friend, family member, colleague, acquaintance, child, son or daughter, or even romantic partner. As empaths, we have the unfortunate tendency to attract energy vampires into our lives because of our innate desire to help and heal people. Because energy vampires generally lack emotional maturity, they tend to feed off others in an attempt to heal their deep inner pain or insecurities. In other words, energy vampires are attracted to us because they unconsciously desire to resolve a deeper problem within their lives, and they perceive *us* as the solution to their problems. While mature empaths may have no problem dealing with energy vampires, untrained empaths may struggle because of a lack of personal boundaries.

Showing Compassion to Energy Vampires

The term "energy vampire" itself is a useful label to identify people in our lives who drain our energy, but such a term can also trigger a lot of resentment and prejudice within us. After all, these people are draining our life force energy! Not only that, but they seem to have little regard for us at all or how *we* feel, making us feel completely used. Therefore, it seems justifiable to call them "vampires."

While it's easy to feel animosity towards energy vampires, we need to remember that these are people who haven't developed the capacity to deal with their issues yet. Energy vampires prey on others because they are in pain, and their behavior is a disguised cry for help. However, the important thing to remember is that you are *not* responsible for resolving their issues. While you can offer help to an energy vampire, it is ultimately *their* responsibility to sort out their struggles.

Therefore, showing compassion to energy vampires is about realizing that they're people in a lot of pain, but they're also ultimately responsible for themselves. This distinction helps us to create and maintain our own boundaries so that we don't end up overextending ourselves and becoming sick.

As Ella, an empath reader on our blog elegantly wrote, "The moment I realized that I wasn't actually responsible for other's well-being, I felt completely liberated and my whole perception of responsibility and helping others was changed. There's this great saying that goes, 'You can lead the horse to the river but you can't force it to drink.' I always keep this in mind now because I don't want to waste my energies trying to help people who aren't willing to help themselves. This has been one of the most important lessons of my life."

How to Identify an Energy Vampire

So how can you identify the presence of an energy vampire in your life? Some of the most common telltale signs you've come in contact with an energy vampire include the following feelings:

- Feeling overwhelmed
- Feeling stressed
- Suffering from physical illness (e.g. headaches, body aches, etc.)
- Feeling mentally or physically exhausted
- Feeling irritable and/or anxious

You may also notice that energy vampires display many of the following characteristics:

- Big ego, e.g. loves to debate, argue and pick fights
- Aggressive or passive-aggressive tendencies
- Paranoia
- Resentment and anger issues
- Self-centeredness
- Melodramatic behavior
- Whining and complaining

123

- Bitching and gossiping
- Insecurity, e.g. the constant need for reassurance and acceptance
- Manipulative behaviors, e.g. guilt tripping, emotional blackmail etc.
- Jealousy

Energy Vampires are, in most cases, takers rather than givers who enjoy talking about themselves and their problems at every given opportunity.

It's also good to realize that energy vampires are not always necessarily human beings. They can also be situations or even physical objects in your life that drain your energy. Examples include the internet, the television, other electronic devices (e.g. the radio, mobile phone, etc.), public situations (e.g. crowds, parties, train stations, shopping centers etc.), and even animals (e.g. neurotic pets).

Types of Energy Vampires

Within the human realm, there are actually a number of different types of energy vampires. See how many you've met:

1. The victim or martyr vampire

Victim or martyr energy vampires prey off your guilt and sincerely believe they are "at the mercy" of the world, suffering primarily due to other people. Instead of taking self-responsibility for their lives, victim/martyr vampires continually blame, manipulate and emotionally blackmail others. The dysfunctional behavior of the victim/martyr vampire is due to their extremely low self-esteem. Without always receiving signs of love, thanks, and approval, victim/martyr vampires

124

feel unworthy and unacceptable, which are feelings they try to resolve by making you feel guilty or feeding off your sympathy and empathy.

2. The egotistical vampire

Egotistical energy vampires have little genuine interest or empathy towards other people, and they carry around the unconscious philosophy of "ME first, YOU second." Therefore, egotistical vampires will constantly expect you to put them first, feed their egos, and do what they say. Egotistical vampires will also manipulate you with false charm, but will just as quickly turn around and stab you in the back. If you have an egotistical vampire in your life, you might feel a sense of extreme disempowerment as you feel crushed beneath their limelight. In this sense, egotistical vampires overlap with a lot of narcissistic qualities.

3. The dominator vampire

Dominator energy vampires love to feel superior to others and like "alpha" males or females. Due to their deep inner insecurities of being "weak" or "wrong" (and therefore hurt), dominator vampires must overcompensate by intimidating you. Dominator vampires are usually loud-mouthed types of people who have rigid beliefs and black and white perceptions of the world. They are often racist, sexist, homophobic, and/or bigoted.

4. The melodramatic vampire

The melodramatic energy vampire thrives on creating problems. Often, their need to create constant drama is a product of a dark underlying emptiness in their lives.

Melodramatic vampires also love seeking out crisis because it gives them a reason to feel victimized (thus special and in need of love), as well as an exaggerated sense of self-importance and avoidance from life's real issues. Another reason why melodramatic vampires enjoy creating drama is that the negative emotions that they feed off are addictive (such as anger).

5. The judgmental vampire

Due to their severely low self-worth, the judgmental energy vampire loves to bully other people. However, their treatment of others is merely a reflection of how they treat themselves. Judgmental vampires enjoy preying on your insecurities and bolstering their egos by making you feel small, pathetic or ashamed.

6. The innocent vampire

Energy vampires aren't always malicious, as in the case of innocent vampires. Sometimes, energy vampires can be helpless types of people who genuinely need help such as children or good friends who come to rely on you and your energy too much.

How to Reduce Empathic Fatigue From Energy Vampires

As we can see, energy vampires come in all shapes and sizes. And if we're honest with ourselves, we've likely displayed energy vampirism at some point in our lives as well. But while most people have played the energy vampire role at a certain time or another, the real issues occur when we meet a person who consistently feeds off the energy of others. Indeed, feeding off energy can actually become an addiction, so we have to be careful that we don't end up becoming the "drug" of choice used by others.

While it's good that we help those who come to us in need, it's also important that we encourage these people to be self-sufficient.

Here are some of the best ways to approach energy vampire connections as an empath:

1. Reduce prolonged eye contact.

I've personally found that prolonged eye contact is one of the biggest energy absorbers. The more eye-contact you make, the more you engage with the other person and what they have to say. Only occasional eye-contact is necessary when you're engaging with an extreme energy vampire.

2. Set a time limit.

Your time is precious, and it's not necessary for you to sit around for one or two hours having your energy zapped and brain numbed. According to your energy level, set a limit of five to ten minutes where you can give your focus to the person, and don't break that time limit.

3. Learn not to react.

Not reacting to what an energy vampire says is very important because they tend to feed off your reactions, fueling them to continue interacting with you. Therefore, it's essential for you to learn how to be neutral in your interactions, meaning that you need to learn how to mindfully filter your positive and negative emotions before you express them.

4. Don't argue with them.

Yes it's tempting to argue with some energy vampires, but in the long run you can't change other people unless they change themselves first. Therefore, the more you resist them, the more they will resist (and drain) you.

5. Go with other people.

Approaching the energy vampire with one, two or three other people will help decrease the level of effort you have to expend. For this tip to work, you need to ensure that the additional people aren't psychic leeches either!

6. Listen more than talk.

Listening more than talking might come naturally to you, or perhaps it doesn't. In any case, energy vampires are usually only seeking for people to listen to them. The more you talk, the more energy you tend to lose (especially if you're introverted). Using questions that involve the words "why?" "when?" and "how?" will encourage the energy vampire to do most of the talking, which in turn will help preserve your energy.

7. Try sticking to light-hearted topics.

Your conversations don't always need to be oppressive. Take control when necessary and change the topic of conversation to something more light and simple.

8. Breathe deeply.

Stay centered in the presence of an energy vampire by paying attention to your breath and breathing deeply. The more air flows within your body, the more energy you will have, and the more grounded you will be.

9. Remember that you aren't there to fix their issues.

As an empath, it's in your nature to want to listen to, empathize with, support, and help others, and you should respect this. But it's important that you also realize that it's not your place to solve or fix an energy vampire's problems, no matter how much they may convince you that it is. Realizing that it's ultimately up to the energy vampire to take self-responsibility for their happiness will emotionally free you from the unnecessary burden of carrying their suffering.

10. Cut off contact.

Cutting off contact with the energy vampire is the last resort. Sometimes, for your own health and happiness, you need to make difficult decisions regarding whom you choose to surround yourself with, and whom you decide to distance yourself from. In the end, if you're still continuing to suffer, the best option may be to simply cut ties and move on.

We'll explore other ways of preserving your energy in later chapters.

Psychic Attack

One prevalent issue linked to energy vampires is that of "psychic attack." Psychic attack is a term that refers to negative energy that a person sends with the conscious or unconscious intention to inflict harm upon you and your life.

Specifically, this malicious energy is directed towards sabotaging your physical, mental, emotional, or spiritual well-being. Many new age practitioners out there suggest that psychic attack comes not only from other people, but also from entities such as spirits, ghosts, or demons. But generally speaking, psychic attack is said to happen when another human being feels and directs emotions such as anger, hatred, resentment, jealousy and other negative emotions towards you, resulting in you experiencing a range of negative consequences. Common symptoms associated with psychic attack include frightening dreams, headaches, unexplained illnesses, extreme mood swings, exhaustion, sleep paralysis, and feeling cursed, watched, or physically controlled. Other signs can include dirty looks, bad luck, unusual fights with others, or people suddenly turning against you for no reason.

As we can see, psychic attack is a concept that generates tremendous amounts of fear and paranoia within us as empaths. But what can we do about this issue? Firstly, we need to realize that while psychic attack is a reality of life, we don't need to be scared of it or give away our power. In fact, it is our fear of being psychically attacked that creates our suffering. As empaths, we need to understand that psychic attack is primarily negative energy that a person intentionally throws at us, but it is up to us to stand firm and not allow this energy to have any real impact on us. Yes, it is in our nature to feel the darkest and most hateful emotions and intentions transmitted by others, but it is our choice to attach to this energy and suffer. No one can make us suffer without our consent. As the famous and wise saying commonly attributed to Buddha goes, "Pain is inevitable, but suffering is optional." In other words, while we are destined to feel the pain of other's darkness, it is our choice to suffer as a result of feeling this pain.

Instead of resisting the energy of psychic attack, it is much better just to acknowledge it, breathe through it, and let it go. The more we resist energy, the more it amplifies and builds in intensity. Therefore, it's much better just to surrender and realize that the pain you're experiencing is temporary. While there are so many practices in the rest of this book that can help you deal with psychic attack, here are a few recommendations:

- Remember that you're only powerless when *you believe* that you're powerless.
- Breathe through the anxiety, anger, confusion, or other emotions that you're experiencing mindfully. Stop everything that you're doing and focus on your in-breath and out-breath for five minutes.
- Ask yourself, "Am I projecting my emotions onto another person?" Sometimes we mistakenly believe that another person is psychically attacking us when in reality, it is our *own* disowned emotional energy that is attacking us.
- Be careful of using psychic attack as an excuse to bypass responsibility for your happiness. It's easy to blame other people for feeling miserable, but at the end of the day, it is ultimately up to you to proactively work to maintain your well-being.
- Understand that people who intentionally try to harm you do so because they are also suffering. Try to feel compassion for those who wish you were suffering. If you can find it within you, send love and good intentions to those who try to send you darkness. Compassion is an extremely pure and high vibrational type of energy that will make you feel one hundred times better.

- Physically remove yourself from the person or situation. Sometimes physical space can help to interrupt the flow of energy.
- Avoid reacting to the attacking energy. Be still, calm, and aware. Notice any tendency you have towards retaliation and let it go. The more neutral you remain, the more grounded and relaxed you will be.
- Refrain from seeing yourself as a victim. Psychic attack is a major trigger for self-victimization. Don't fall into this trap. The more you feel like a victim, the more you'll buy into the belief that you're powerless — and as I mentioned before, you are only powerless when you believe that you are. Draw on your inner strength. Contact your inner Self through prayer. If necessary, ask for help from loved ones, professionals, or spiritual helpers. You have all the power and resources you need around you. Just take a look around you and right in front of you at this book!
- Be mindful of paranoia. Psychic attack is one of those topics that tends to generate a hugely fearful response in us. Very soon, it's easy for us to start associating every bad experience we go through with psychic attack. Please realize that genuine, calculated psychic attack is extremely uncommon and in most cases, rare. If you are wrestling with paranoid thoughts, please refer to chapter 15.
- Notice resistant thoughts. Thoughts such as, "Why me?" "This is horrible," "I don't want this to happen" only serve to create more resistance and therefore more suffering. Accept the situation rather than ruminating on negative thoughts and look for ways to reaffirm your strength rather than diminish it.

- Visualize white light immersing your entire body. Imagine this white light cleansing and purifying your energy field of any harmful influence.
- Instead of shielding, let go. Shielding is a technique that involves resisting energy in an attempt to "protect" ourselves. However, this is an unsustainable and tiring practice. Not only that but whatever we resist tends to persist. So instead, learn how to let go. When you feel dark or disturbing energy enter your energy field, acknowledge it, let yourself feel it, and then it will naturally dissipate. The easiest way to let go is just to use your breath to "breathe out" the energy within you. You might also like to try visualizing the energy leaving your body (please see the Sending Back Energy Visualization in chapter 16).

If you ever experience psychic attack at any point in the future, please remember that you always have a choice. You have a choice between perceiving yourself as a powerless victim or an empowered empath. While the powerless victim experiences suffering because they believe they've got no choice, the empowered empath experiences pain, but does not allow that pain to harm them. By practicing non-resistance, mindfulness, compassion, and surrender, fear has no place in our hearts.

Creating Balance

Personally, I've never really liked the term "energy vampire," but it is a useful phrase that can help us identify people in our lives who drain large amounts of energy from us. When it comes to our connection with energy vampires, we need to realize that, as empaths, energy exchange is a dance. In other words, it takes two to tango. Thus, an energy vampire can never "steal" energy from us unless we consciously or unconsciously permit them to.

As children, many of us were taught that self-sacrifice was a noble virtue, which is why many of us empaths feel selfish in our desire to keep some of our energy for ourselves. But without respecting our energetic boundaries, it is impossible for us to give quality and sustained caring attention to the people in our lives who need it the most.

Facing and seeing through the mistaken beliefs we inherited as children is vital if we're to ever learn how to create balance in our lives. In fact, learning how to take responsibility for our energy is the best gift we can give to future generations, and in particular, to our children.

Chapter 12 – Parenting Empath Children

Childhood can be the single greatest and most difficult period for us as empaths.

During our years of development, we have no concept of boundaries, no capacity to determine if the happiness of others is our responsibility, and little ability to take care of our own needs. Overall, we are completely at the mercy of our parents', teachers', and peers' expectations.

While all children are completely vulnerable to their surroundings, being born as a highly sensitive empath amplifies all of these difficulties ten-fold. The sheer quantity of energy and information bombarding the empath child's senses tends to overwhelm them very quickly, resulting in behavioral issues and illnesses that are often misdiagnosed. Not only that, but empathic children are more susceptible to developing problems such as anxiety and depression in later life,[1] especially if they experience emotionally turbulent upbringings.[2]

Picture this: You're a child again and you've just been picked up by your mother. Imagine that she's had a hard day at work, and she's visibly tired and irritable. Suddenly, you do something that upsets her, and she lashes out at you in anger. "Stop being an idiot! You're driving me *crazy*. Sit down RIGHT NOW or I'll give you a smack." Shocked, you sit down. What you have done doesn't justify the amount of anger that's been shot at you. But as an empath, you can feel what your mother is feeling, and therefore learn to believe her when she angrily tells you that you're "stupid," "clumsy," "useless," or "bad."

Through time, you internalize these beliefs, and learn to completely ignore how *you* feel.

While small moments of anger such as these may not seem like much, such moments over time tend to form negative core beliefs and wounds that eventually shape the empath child's self-image. Unless we actively work to explore and heal these inner wounds that developed in childhood, our lives tend to be run by them behind the scenes. In chapter 15, we'll explore numerous ways to compassionately deal with these harmful core beliefs.

In this chapter, we'll explore how to thrive and flourish as an empathic parent juggling the endless responsibilities of parenthood. We'll also later explore how to lovingly and mindfully raise empathic children in today's bustling and often insensitive world. Even if your child isn't an empath, you'll find that much of the advice is offered here is still valuable to your child (or children) on an emotional level.

Advice For Empath Parents

Parenting for empaths is a deeply rewarding but extraordinarily intense experience. On one hand we get to vicariously live through the eyes of our beloved children, feel love constantly radiating from our hearts, and witness the growth of these precious beings of light. For many empath parents, parenting is like living a second childhood where life is suddenly full of wonder again. On the other hand, we tend to feel on the verge of hysteria and burnout with the screaming, crying, demanding, and time consuming duties that come with raising a child. Not only that, but juggling child-rearing with work, relationship, friendship, and family responsibilities can easily overwhelm us.

How can we thrive as sensitive parents? How can we balance our own needs *and* the needs of our children?

Here are some tools and tips you can use to find inner calm and reduce sensory overload.

1. Breathe consciously and practice witnessing.

When our children throw tantrums and become angry, sad or scared we are prone to absorbing these emotions into our bodies. Instead of getting wound up in these feelings, practice breathing deeply and "witnessing" the emotions within you. Witnessing is a practice that originated in ancient Hindu spiritual philosophy, and it involves observing whatever arises inside of you. Instead of getting caught in the vortex of the emotions within you, anchor yourself to your breath, and watch the feelings in a detached manner. Later, in chapter 17, we'll share with you a technique called SOAR that can help you practice witnessing.

2. Create pockets of solitude.

It is absolutely imperative to make alone time as an empathic parent. Without finding time to unwind and reconnect with yourself in solitude, your nervous system will fry very easily. Even just ten minutes a day of complete solitude is enough to help you recover from the demands of parenting. If you're a stay at home parent, find solace during your children's nap times. Also, if you have supportive friends or family members, enlist their help to mind your child while you take some time off. You might even like to set up a "care plan" with your partner so that each of you get to spend time alone to rest.

3. Learn to say "no."

Empaths tend to make over-vigilant caregivers of their children, so saying "no" can be a big struggle. Because we feel our children's emotions, we are quick to appease their demands and requests. In order to create balance, we need to learn how to distinguish between our child's needs and wants. While a child's needs are vital, their wants aren't always necessary. It's OK to gently and firmly say "no" when they are demanding too much.

4. Maintain a soothing atmosphere.

Create "good vibes" in your house by choosing color schemes and other items that will help soothe your children. When the atmosphere is relaxed, your children will calm down because they are very receptive to energy. Play soothing ocean sounds as an immediate way to soothe your children.

5. Prepare wholesome food.

Children become hyperactive and destructive when they are fed food that contains colors, flavors, preservatives, and other artificial additives. Try incorporating whole grains, fruits, vegetables, nuts, and legumes into your child's diet. If you're lacking time, set aside a couple of spare hours to bulk prepare your food for the whole week. Freeze whatever you aren't going to immediately use.

6. Take naps.

If you're a stay at home parent, take advantage of your child's nap times and rest at the same time. Parenting can be exhausting, so give yourself the permission to rest, recuperate, and regain your energy.

7. Avoid micromanaging.

Although we have good intentions, sometimes we are a little too enthusiastic and tend to smother our children. Because we are highly intuitive and can pick up on our children's needs, we may become overly anxious and excessively involved in our children's lives. To avoid being a "helicopter parent," learn to let go and trust in your child's abilities. By letting go, you will also reduce your own stress level and support your child in building self-confidence.

8. Be mindful of your energy.

Whatever energy you're transmitting will influence your child, so if you are feeling stressed out, your child will also become stressed out ... and this equals even more stress! By being mindful of your energy and finding ways to become grounded again, you will stop anxiety building within yourself and your child. Children are more receptive to our energy than we think. You'll discover a range of grounding practices in chapter 14.

9. Let love and laughter uplift you.

When we're feeling tired, stressed, and cranky, it can be easy to develop a negative mindset and start dwelling on annoyances. To counteract this tendency, focus on the privileges of parenting and how blessed you are to raise such beautiful children. By choosing to revel in the awe, joy, and laughter your children bring, your household will radiate with warmth and love. Love and laughter are two of the most powerful forces to counteract feelings of stress and inundation.

By incorporating this advice into your life, you will be able to find more balance, serenity, and bliss as an empath parent.

Signs Your Child is an Empath

If being an empath is draining for adults, just imagine what it must feel like for a child that doesn't have the language or capacity to explain what they're experiencing to others! For this reason, empath children often express themselves through varying forms of frustration.

Here are some external signs that you should look out for in your child. Keep in mind that the younger your child is, the more difficult it will be to determine whether or not they are an empath:

- Unexplained tantrums
- Crying or laughing when other people cry or laugh
- They finish your sentences as if they can read your thoughts
- Chronic sickness like colds, flus, asthma, anemia, stomach upset, etc.
- They love being in nature and around animals
- They are disturbed by strong smells, noises, tastes, textures, etc.
- They have a small number of friends instead of a large playgroup
- They act out when you're stressed, depressed or angry
- Extreme shifts in moods or behavior
- Sharing that they feel "different" or "weird"
- They share surprising intuitive comments about you or others
- They might appear emotionally distant or "shut down" when too much is going on
- You constantly find them preferring to spend time alone in solitude away from others

- They display an excessive concern for the problems of adults
- Difficulties focusing, especially when they are in public or crowded places

By themselves, many of these signs could have several explanations. However, when several of the signs above appear together repeatedly, it is likely that you have an empathic child.

Indigo Children

Unsurprisingly, many empath children are also highly intuitive old souls. These types of kids are called "Indigo Children"; a concept developed in the 1970s which refers to a group of individuals who have come to this earth to create change. Those who identify as indigo empaths, and possess kids who share indigo traits, share that they have always felt like this world is not their true home. Some authors speculate that indigo children have lived many lifetimes and have come to this earth with a profound understanding of the human condition. Aleksandra, a reader of ours, for example, shared a story about her son, who displays qualities of being an indigo child, "Ever since Daniel was little he has known things I've never spoken about, like how his grandmother died or one of the pets we had before he was born. He asks me questions like, 'Mommy, why is everyone pretending? They seem so angry and sad' and points out things like 'He's lying to you, don't you know?' He also remembers things about the 'other Daniels' that he used to be. It's all very strange. I've been told he's a new wave indigo child."

While the concept of indigo children has never been proven, it could explain why so many empaths possess intriguing spiritual gifts and don't fit in with other kids.

Are you, or is your child, an indigo empath? Here are some of the most common signs:

- Highly sensitive and intuitive
- Possess extrasensory gifts like clairvoyance and precognition
- Strong-willed
- Gets bored easily
- Freethinking and questions rules and authority that are outdated
- Tremendous desire to be of help to humanity
- Empathetic and compassionate
- Highly intelligent
- Free-spirited and find it hard to fit into "normal" society
- Visionary
- Interest in protecting, healing, nurturing, and advocating for other living beings such as the earth, animals, minorities, etc.
- Very perceptive and insightful about the human condition
- Feel like they have a major life purpose

Indigo empaths are also old souls who tend to display surprising maturity and wisdom for their age. I explore the topic of old souls more in my book *Old Souls: The Sages and Mystics of Our World.*

How to Care For Empath Children

142

It is speculated that the gift of being an empath is inherited as a genetic trait that is passed down through generations. If this is the case, it is likely that your child (or children) share the same finely-tuned gift that one of your parents or grandparents also had.

While a large percentage of children are born sensitive and empathic, they quickly learn through harsh experiences and media exposure to desensitize themselves to avoid the pain that high sensitivity can bring. This protection mechanism of "shutting off" sensitivity is sadly even encouraged by our societies, with remarks such as "toughen up," "get thicker skin," and "you're too sensitive" constantly being propagated. The thing is, not all empaths can completely numb and desensitize themselves, so they are often open for attack. By "attack," I don't just mean physical attacks, but also non-physical and passive attacks such as screaming, name calling, passive aggressive jokes, belittling jabs, accusations, and arrogant disregard. Some empath children also become the scapegoats for their family's anger, sadness, and resentment, especially if the family is largely emotionally immature or stunted. Because the empath child is seen as being "strange" or "different" from the rest of the family, they receive the brunt of the family's projected and repressed emotions.

With energies such as hostility, despair, and fear constantly floating in the air, it's no wonder that empath children often get diagnosed with neurological or psychological disorders such as ADHD, OCD, MPD, and social anxiety disorder. The influx of intense energy they constantly receive is often too much to handle, so dysfunctional self-protection strategies are developed.

If you are the parent of an empath child, it is your sacred responsibility to understand, accept, and nurture your child in ways that suit him or her best. Parents of empath children often struggle to truly tune into their child's delicate needs, especially in a society that is obsessed with telling us how we "should" and "shouldn't" raise our children. However, once we can stop and truly connect to the heart of our child, our own authentic parenting style will naturally develop and blossom.

While all empath children are different and require slightly different parenting styles, there are some pieces of advice that are timeless and universal:

1. Understand and acknowledge your child's high receptivity.

It's important that you take the time to understand and accept your child's sensitive abilities. Telling them that they are "too sensitive" or making them "push through" their emotions is not the answer. By learning to be present with your child, you'll begin listening to how they're truly feeling, and therefore help them feel accepted and understood.

2. Help them to feel empowered by their gift.

Too many empaths end up growing into adults who feel like there's something innately wrong with them due to constant rejection as children. In order to prevent this from happening to your child, help them to understand that their sensitivity is a valuable gift to have. Let them know that some people won't understand them, and that is normal to feel different. No matter what anyone says, help them to see that they are perfect just as they are. You might even like to explain how their sensitivity makes them kind, loving, intelligent, and thoughtful, and that it's OK to feel tired or sad around others. You could even say that feeling other people's emotions is like having a cool superpower like x-ray vision. It's important that your child feels that they aren't broken due to their differences, and that you are always there to help them.

3. Teach them to tune into feelings.

Because your child can so easily feel other people's emotions, it's important that you teach them to not neglect their *own* emotions, which can lead to serious issues further down the line. When they are angry or stressed, for example, teach them to take time out in a quiet place alone. Encourage them to cry when they feel sad and to release any anger they have in healthy ways, such as through sport, dancing, writing or different forms of art. By encouraging them to release the emotional energy they absorb, you will help them to feel happier and healthier.

4. Teach them that not everything is their responsibility.

The word responsibility is composed of two separate words, response and ability, or the ability to respond.

Empath children at such a tender age aren't fully capable of responding in a mature way to the struggles around them. Because your child is so sensitive, they will deeply perceive and understand the motivations, needs, choices, and actions of the people around them, and therefore try to do their best to help. However, the more your child "takes responsibility" for negative emotions and situations, the more they will suffer.

Your child will benefit a lot if you teach them that they aren't responsible for other people's happiness or for fulfilling their every need. Although it is nice to help others, remind your child that they need to take care of their needs as well. Help them to identify when they're feeling exhausted and overwhelmed, and remind them that they can only truly help others when they help themselves. For example, depending on how old they are, you might like to teach them affirmations such as "I'm only responsible for my feelings," "It's OK to take a break," and "I will go at my own pace."

If your child is a teenage empath, you might like to try introducing them to self-inquiry. As sensitive beings, empathic teenagers struggle greatly to differentiate their emotions from those around them. One of the best ways to help your child regulate their emotions is by teaching them to ask, "Is this feeling mine?" Self-inquiry like this, when made into a habit, can help your child gain more clarity and inner balance knowing that they aren't responsible for everyone else's feelings. (For teenage children, you might even like to lend them a copy of this book for further guidance.)

5. Give them space to be themselves.

Allow your child to dislike being around certain people. If they want to be alone, give them the space to be alone. Be careful of trying to force them to be a certain way (i.e. "social") when what they might really need is time to decompress. Many parents, unfortunately, force their children to pursue extracurricular and social commitments that drain their children's energy. Permit your child to be him or herself. Give them the freedom to choose from many options.

6. Emotionally stabilize your household.

Empath children are highly influenced by the energy of the household, including the energy of you as a parent. This means that your child will be perceptive of your moods and will feel everything that you feel, regardless of whether you want them to or not. Empath children are also extremely sensitive to arguing and yelling, which deeply disturbs them on a physical and emotional level.

The best way to prevent your child from absorbing your emotions is to make it your goal to stay as centered as possible. Learning to stay centered might mean taking up practices such as meditation, yoga, or mindfulness to help you peacefully process the anxiety, anger, or sadness you may be feeling. By being aware, you will help to create a calm environment for your child to thrive in. You can find more exercises for creating emotional stability in chapter 16.

7. Communicate with them when something is wrong.

We may not be aware of it, but empath children are highly perceptive of everything that goes around them. They can sense when something is off and will feel your troubled energy. Because they don't know the source of your turbulent emotions, they often tend to wind up feeling like they are somehow responsible. To prevent this misunderstanding from happening, simply tell your child when something has gone wrong. You don't have to share all the details, but do let them know why you're feeling anxious, frustrated or depressed. For example, you might like to tell your child that "Mommy received some bad news so she's feeling sad" or "Daddy is tired so he's feeling cranky today." It's amazing how simple this strategy is, but it works.

8. Be an advocate for your child.

Educate your child's teachers and other family members about their sensitivity and tendency to experience sensory overload. Be aware that others have very different ideas about your child and who they "should" be, so be prepared to respond in a mature (and non-reactive) way, even if this means gritting your teeth and fuming internally! Do not allow anyone to bully, judge, or criticize your child, no matter who they are. Show your child that you support them and will defend their needs in a loving, firm, and mature way. Doing so will help your child feel safe and honored.

9. Create a calm physical space.

Empath children need space to wind down and relax due to their overactive nervous systems. Try to create calm spaces in your house that are disconnected from technology and other distractions. You might like to choose a dark and quiet place which soothes the nervous system and put indoor plants, candles, pillows, oil burners, or other items that encourage relaxation in this area.

10. Teach them how to work with their gift.

Some further ways to help your empathic child include:

- Ensuring you set stable bedtimes that allow at least 8 hours of solid, rejuvenating sleep.
- Encouraging them to spend plenty of time in nature. Ecotherapy is a powerful way to help them ground and recharge their energy.
- Teaching them relaxation techniques such as breathing deeply, visualizing, blowing bubbles, doing meditation

and yoga, praying, etc. Teenagers, for example, are better suited to meditation practices, and younger children may benefit more from simple breathing exercises.

- Reducing their exposure to stimulating situations which burn them out.
- Reducing their exposure to violent video games and TV shows.
- Helping them to identify and be assertive around energy vampires. Teach them how to say "no" in a kind and gentle way, and to stay away from angry people. If your child can't avoid a person, teach them how to breathe deeply in order to stay grounded and to let the emotions pass through them.

The feelings that empathic children absorb from others can often be overwhelming, scary, and confusing for them. But by listening to them, empowering them, and preparing them for the world, you will help them feel accepted and loved exactly as they are. This is all your child is really looking for at the end of the day.

Chapter 13 – Empaths and the Spiritual Awakening Process

"Humankind has not woven the web of life. We are but one thread within it. Whatever we do to the web, we do to ourselves. All things are bound together. All things connect." – **Chief Seattle**

As empaths, we are like oracles and seers who can feel into the different layers of energetic experience around us. We are not fooled by the facades of others. We are rarely ever deceived. We can sense and inhabit the emotions of others effortlessly. We can feel the intimate mysteries of the heart. Yet our ability to tune into the vibrational reality around us also comes with a flip side: we often feel like complete aliens on this planet. Our high level of sensitivity means that we are prone to feeling like eternal outsiders who are in the world, but not quite of the world. When this feeling of alienation is prolonged, we have the tendency to become deeply depressed.

Empaths and Existential Depression

It's deeply concerning that very few people know about existential depression. Most people assume that all depression is the "same" depression, i.e. depression that is caused by chemical imbalances in the brain, traumatic life experiences or negative thinking patterns. But existential depression is much more mysterious and profound than regular depression.

So what exactly is existential depression? In a nutshell, existential depression is a crisis of the Soul. When we experience existential depression as empaths, we feel an intense and philosophical dissatisfaction with life, and a separation from our very essence. Such a form of depression can be crippling and profound. What mainstream therapist can work to heal a sickness of the Soul? In fact, not much is known about existential depression in the world of psychotherapy. Clinically, existential depression falls into a "grey" area and is often classified as being "uncaused." In other words, psychotherapy has no idea why existential depression occurs at all. As such, it's no surprise that many empaths who seek counselling for this type of depression walk away feeling misunderstood, misdiagnosed or even more depressed than before.

Signs that you have or are currently experiencing existential depression include:

- Continuous "deep thoughts" about the meaning and nature of life
- The intense desire to answer seemingly unanswerable questions such as "What is the purpose of existence?" "What happens after death?" "Why was I born?"
- Intense dissatisfaction with the state of society
- Feeling disconnected from others (thus few or no friends)
- Feeling misunderstood and on a "different level" from others
- Chronic and profound loneliness
- Sensations of being "dead," "numb," or "empty" inside
- Disinterest in social contact because it feels shallow
- Melancholic moods
- Anxiety
- Loss of interest in usual pursuits
- Lack of enthusiasm or motivation

- Low energy
- Belief that most things are "futile" or "meaningless"
- Contemplation or attempt of suicide

As an empath who has struggled with severe existential depression before, and who has helped many others struggling with it, I can tell you that it *is* possible to overcome this deep melancholy, thankfully. But before we emerge from the black waters of existential depression, we need to understand why it has happened to us. While the specific cause or trigger that set off existential depression is always unique, this type of depression itself is a symptom of a larger overarching experience known as the Dark Night of the Soul.

The Dark Night of the Soul

As highly sensitive empaths, we are particularly prone to experiencing the Dark Night of the Soul. The less defined our sense of self is and the more toxic energy we take on from others, the more we are prone to losing touch with our Souls.

You can think of your Soul as the ultimate GPS, or guidance system, within you. Your Soul is the place within you that is timeless, ageless, and eternal: it is the ultimate core and essence of who you truly are. In the modern world, we most frequently come in contact with our Souls through meditation practices. But often, the Soul gently and subtly emerges in our daily lives through synchronicity (strange serendipitous occurrences) and intuition.

When we lose touch with our Souls, we lose touch with our inner guidance, wisdom, and strength. Sometimes, it can take us many years to get back in touch with the divine presence

152

within us. This period of feeling lost and disconnected from the divine is called the Dark Night of the Soul.

I feel that it's important to mention here that the Dark Night of the Soul is not merely "having a bad day" or even week. The Dark Night is a long, pervasive, and very dark experience. If you're experiencing the Dark Night of the Soul, you will constantly carry around within you a sense of being lost. Your heart will constantly, in some shape or form, be in mourning, and this is because you long deep down to feel the presence of your Soul again.

As an empath, you are particularly prone to experiencing the Dark Night of the Soul. Here are seven signs to look out for:

1. You feel a deep sense of sadness which often verges on despair (this sadness is often triggered by the state of your life, humanity, and/or the world as a whole).
2. You feel an acute sense of unworthiness.
3. You have the constant feeling of being lost or "condemned" to a life of suffering or emptiness.
4. You possess a painful feeling of powerlessness and hopelessness.
5. Your will and self-control is weakened, making it difficult for you to act.
6. You lack interest and find no joy in things that once excited you.
7. You crave for the loss of something intangible; you long for a distant place or to "return home" again.

Take a few moments to get silent and tune into your body. Can you resonate with this list of symptoms? Are you experiencing the Dark Night of the Soul?

Although the Dark Night sounds, and feels scary, there is hope. There is a light at the end of the tunnel, and that light is called the Spiritual Awakening Process.

The Spiritual Awakening Process

Mythologist and writer Joseph Campbell once proposed that we all go through what is known as "The Hero's Journey."[1] This mythological journey always begins with a hero who journeys into the unknown in order to reach his or her highest potential. Along the way, this hero encounters enemies, helpers, mentors, and eventually what is known as "the abyss." Once the hero emerges out of the abyss (often called the "darkness"), the hero experiences a spiritual rebirth. Does this journey sound familiar to you?

Almost every story, both fiction and nonfiction, echoes The Hero's Journey. Turn on the television, read a book, or watch a movie, and you will see The Hero's Journey constantly portrayed in thousands of different ways all the time. We empaths also go through our own unique versions of The Hero's Journey. Almost always, our journeys involve experiencing a period of the Dark Night of the Soul. But rather than being a terrible fate, the Dark Night is actually an extremely natural and beneficial process of rebirth. In other words, the Dark Night of the Soul prepares us for the Spiritual Awakening Process.

One of the greatest advantages of being an empath is that experiencing a spiritual awakening is virtually inevitable. In other words, spiritually awakening seems to be written into our individual and collective DNA. Our extreme energetic sensitivity means that it is very hard for us to live in a world of illusion. It is very difficult and simply too painful to continue being separated from our Souls; thus we are destined to eventually "awaken."

So what exactly is the Spiritual Awakening Process? The Spiritual Awakening Process is essentially a sacred rebirth. When we awaken, we begin to crave for an existence that is much deeper than pursuing money, fame or status: we begin to look for our true life purpose. When we awaken, we begin to sense that there is much more to life than physical reality. We begin to realize that happiness cannot be found in external pursuits, but it is something that can only be found within. We begin to listen to our hearts more, not only our heads. We begin to long for spiritual liberation and unification with others. Most of all, we long to embody our Soul, or True Nature. Some of us even search for "enlightenment" or complete spiritual liberation.

Experiencing a spiritual awakening marks the beginning of your initiation on the spiritual path. While the Dark Night of the Soul is a process of death, the Spiritual Awakening Process is the rebirth.

As an empath, you are blessed with the ability to easily shift into higher levels of consciousness. Here are some signs that you might be experiencing a spiritual awakening:

1. You crave more meaning and purpose.
2. You realize that a lot of what you've been taught is a lie (based on fearful beliefs).
3. You feel as though everything you've been working towards is false, and won't bring you happiness.
4. You feel completely lost and alone.
5. You're starting to see through the illusions of society (such as materialism).

155

6. Your empathic abilities are being amplified to a painful degree.
7. You constantly desire to be alone with your own thoughts and feelings.
8. You feel profound compassion towards the human condition.
9. You thirst for authenticity and truth.
10. You're becoming conscious of your destructive habits.
11. You no longer desire to be around people who harm or use you.
12. You're experiencing a lot of anxiety or depression.
13. You desperately want to make the world a better place.
14. You deeply want to understand who you are.
15. You're seeing more synchronicity (meaningful coincidences) appear.
16. Your intuition feels heightened.
17. You want to discover your true nature.
18. You long to be liberated from your suffering.
19. You're beginning to love others unconditionally.
20. You see how sacred and interconnected life is.

These are just some of the endless spiritual awakening symptoms out there. As an empath, you are likely to experience a lot of anxiety during the awakening process, particularly in the beginning stages. In the rest of this book, we'll share with you some unique and powerful techniques which can help you stay grounded during this life-changing process.

The question now is, if you've discovered that you're a spiritually awakened empath, or you would like to initiate this process, what do you do next?

Soulwork

If the Spiritual Awakening Process is the journey, Soulwork is the tool that can help you navigate through this journey.

As I previously mentioned, your Soul is your ultimate guidance system. You can think of your Soul as the compass, map, and destination all in one. Confusing? Yes! But it is difficult for our limited minds to truly conceptualize the Soul because it transcends all thought. The best we can do is put labels on our Souls so that we can understand them better. However, in the end, only you can truly meet and understand your Soul with your heart.

Another analogy is that your Soul is the part of you that is an eternal, wise, and infinitely loving being of light. You may even like to conceptualize your Soul as the "goddess" or "god" within you. However you decide to define your Soul, it is crucial that you learn how to listen to its guidance. Once you listen to your Soul's guidance, you will find that every one of your choices and actions is supported and nourished. The practice of listening to your Soul's guidance is called Soulwork.

Soulwork is the practice of learning how to fully embody your Soul. In other words, quite literally, Soulwork is doing the work of your Soul. The people who have learned how to do the work of their Souls and embody their highest calling through the ages have been referred to as healers, masters, sages, saints, and enlightened beings.

As an empath, you are called to step up and listen your Soul's guidance. You are being called to grow, transform, and let go of all that obscures the light of your inner Presence. Soulwork is about learning how to identify the blockages within you so that you can fulfill your personal destiny and highest calling.

Like the rainbow, each person on this planet has a different "colored" Soul, and therefore, a different destiny. Your Soul will "look" and feel much different from another person's Soul, but fundamentally, your Soul is an expression of Spirit, or that which is eternal. Therefore, while all of our destinies are unique and different from others, our overarching purpose as a species is to grow, physically, emotionally, and spiritually. The only way we can experience true spiritual growth is by uniting with our Souls again and doing our Soulwork.

At its core Soulwork always consists of the following three elements, but these elements can often stand alone:

1. Looking – searching for, identifying, understanding or defining the problem.
2. Loving – embracing, accepting, holding, or being unconditionally loving with the pain.
3. Letting Go – letting go of mental stories that create suffering, releasing attachment to ideas and expectations, and surrendering.

When used in conjunction with each other, looking, loving, and letting go form the powerful basis of all Soulwork practice. In the following chapters we'll explore together different techniques that reflect the Soulwork philosophy of Look, Love, Let Go.

Chapter 14 – Healing the Physical Realm

The first step in your journey of healing and empowerment as an empath is focusing on the physical realm. By the "physical realm," I am referring to your body, nervous system, and all related processes within you that are grounded in three-dimensional reality. After learning how to cleanse, center, and relax your body, you will then be able to move onto healing the mental, emotional, and spiritual realms that are covered in the next few chapters.

Doing your personal Soulwork is about learning how to listen to the voice within you. In the next few sections within this chapter, try to pay attention to this subtle voice and what practices you are intuitively drawn towards. Remember, not every practice will appeal to you right now, and that is OK. If you're ever in need of guidance, you can always refer back to the many holistic techniques referred to in this chapter.

Some of the practices written about in this chapter reflect the Soulwork philosophy of Look, Love, Let Go. However, other practices can be thought of as complementary tools that will enhance your wellbeing. Remember that all true healing comes from within, and that also goes for physical healing! So it's important that you don't get too caught up in the technique or the pressure of practicing them all religiously. Do whatever comes naturally to you and be gentle with yourself. Even using one simple technique in this chapter will improve your life as an empath.

Finally, as this chapter will be much longer than other chapters, please take your time and pause where you need to.

Each section is broken down into subheadings to make the information easier for you to digest.

Practice 1 – Detox Your Life

Within the chaos, business, and clutter of everyday life it is very easy for us to lapse into bad habits. These bad habits exacerbate our tendency to feel overwhelmed and inundated by other people's energy, increasing the risk of anxiety and stress-related illnesses. One of the simplest and easiest ways to initiate change in your life is to go through a physical detox. When most people hear the word "detox" they picture cliché smoothie diets, but I promise that I'm not referring to that!

A detox is basically the process of removing unhelpful, unwanted or toxic habits from your life systematically. In other words, a detox is a period of time when you attempt to get yourself "clean" of unwanted habits (kind of like rehab, but less drastic). However, while detoxes are proactive ways to create change, most people don't truly benefit from them. Why? The answer is that detoxes are often fueled by guilt and fail to truly uproot bad habits. How many times have you heard someone say that they're going on a detox after a period of binge-eating? In order for your empathic detox to be effective, you need to firstly approach it with an open mindset and the willingness to *replace* your old habits. By replacing your old habits, you'll be able to introduce more balance into your life.

Remember that detoxes take a while. It's much better to slowly wean yourself off certain habits than aggressively changing everything all at once. Give yourself time to adjust.

Here are four of the top physical ways you can detox your life as an empath:

160

1. Change what you eat.

Yes, this might be obvious. But food carries energy, and as an energy-sensitive person, you are deeply impacted by the food you eat. There is food that nourishes the body and food that makes the body weak, addicted, and sick. If you are in the habit of eating a lot of food that is processed, full of saturated fat, sugar, artificial sweeteners, preservatives, and salt, try to cut back. Your body was not made to consume fake factory food. Your body was made to consume wholesome foods such as fruits, vegetables, whole grains, and legumes. As an empath, you will almost immediately be able to tell the difference in your body. While your body may go through withdrawal symptoms, after a while, you will feel more vibrant, energized, and relaxed. An empath friend once told me ecstatically, "I feel ALIVE now!" after making this simple change. You might also like to consider reducing or cutting out meat and animal products. As an empath, you can pick up on and absorb the energy of not only human beings, but also animals. Eating animals that were pumped full of hormones, locked away in cages or subjected to cruel slaughter has a tendency to impact your energy on a deeper level than you may be aware.

2. Declutter your house.

The reality is that mess causes stress. A study conducted by neuroscientists at Princeton University in 2011 found that physical clutter in your surroundings psychologically competes for your attention.[1] The result is decreased ability to focus and increased stress. And it seems pretty obvious: the more "stuff" you have, the more stuff you have to worry about. The energetic debris from old stuff gathering dust around you has a way of weighing down your energy field. While you don't have to become a minimalist, you can work to simplify your external life, and therefore encourage internal balance. The best place to start is generally with your own personal items. What clothes, shoes, books, utensils, hoarded away items, or trinkets could you best do without? Make a goal to sell, recycle or donate whatever you no longer need. Replace your habit of collecting stuff with the habit of keeping a clean and organized environment. Plus, the less stuff you have, the less cleaning! Enjoy the feeling of having a clean, clear, and organized space, and the newfound clarity it gives you.

3. Remove toxic personal care products.

As an empath, your physical environment impacts your well-being just as much as the people you meet or the thoughts you entertain. According to the Environmental Health Association of Novia Scotia, there are 10,000 ingredients out there that are used in personal products – and the average woman wears 515 of these ingredients each day.[2] Not only that, but more than 90% of these chemicals have never been tested for their impact on human health. Only 7% of ingredients have complete data available for us. Of those ingredients that have been tested, many of them have been found to trigger issues such as asthma, cellular damage, allergic reactions, gene mutations, organ damage, endocrine disruption, and even cancer. In fact, let's try an experiment. Go and read the ingredients on the back of your shampoo or hand lotion bottle right now. Likely, you'll find a long list of ingredients, many of which you can't even pronounce!

As empaths, we need to be concerned about what is going into our bodies. By removing toxic personal care products that contain harmful chemicals such as parabens, phthalates, and sodium laureth sulfate (SLS) we can help our bodies get back in balance. The more balanced our bodies are, the better equipped we'll be to stay grounded as empaths. All toxic shampoos, conditioners, moisturizers, deodorants, creams, perfumes, lotions, nail polish, makeup, and cleaning products have alternatives these days. Simply do a bit of research, and you can find many natural alternatives, some of which you can make (which will save you a lot of money!).

4. Use color psychology and revamp your clothing.

Color is vibration and it impacts our mood significantly. Have you ever wondered why advertisements often use the color red? Red triggers parts of your brain associated with alertness and action. On the other hand, have you ever wondered why hospitals usually have either white or blue walls? These two colors trigger feelings of calmness, trust, positivity, and purity.

The colors you choose and wear each day impact your mood massively. Have you ever wondered why depressed people wear black? Black is associated with negativity, anonymity, and death. In fact, most people intuitively understand the meaning of different colors, but even though we know that colors impact us, we don't seem to apply color psychology to our lives.

Let's try an experiment. Go now and peek into your wardrobe. What is the dominant color you see? If your answer is black or grey, it is time to revamp your clothing choices.

As an empath it's important that you create a supportive environment for yourself, and that includes the choice of color you wear. Often, wearing dark and murky colors actually contributes indirectly to the emotional muddiness you absorb from others. But thankfully, you don't need to go out and buy an entire new wardrobe if you tend to dress yourself in dark colors. You also don't need to dress flamboyantly or like a hippy. Simply choose colors from the clothing you already have, selectively. If you need a few more choices, try a local thrift shop or the sales section of your favorite store. Try to choose colors that are uplifting, grounding, and calming such as green, yellow, blue, purple, violet, pink, orange, and other variations such as turquoise, gold, lavender, and lime. Avoid wearing too much black, grey, brown, or murky colors such as khaki and tan (unless you are positively emotionally impacted by any of these colors). Remember that there are no rules here. These are just suggestions. "Detoxing" your wardrobe is a simple but surprisingly powerful way to infuse a bit more energy and serenity into your day.

We'll explore more serious forms of detox (such as removing toxic people from your life) further on in this book.

Practice 2 – Establish a daily grounding practice.

Making space for a daily grounding practice is practically *essential* as an empath. Our tendency to soak up excess energy from our environments means that it's essential for us to find a way to anchor ourselves back to planet earth again. Grounding also helps us to expel, cleanse, and purify the energy we carry within us.

Here are some of the best daily grounding practices you can experiment with:

- **Spending time in nature.** Nature is the ultimate place for us energy-sensitive people to unwind. The ebb and flow of nature has a way of grounding us back into our bodies, and connecting us with our authentic selves.

- **"Earthing."** Earthing is a more active form of spending time in nature. This practice involves walking barefoot on the earth and allowing the soil to soak up the negative energy in your body. Try to spend ten minutes or more each day earthing. Sit, stand, lay or walk on the soil, grass, or sand, and allow the earth's energies to neutralize your body's energies.
- **Yoga, Tai Chi or Qigong.** Yoga, tai chi, and qigong are all ancient healing therapies that help to circulate the body's Qi or Prana – also known as our life force energy. There are many local yoga, tai chi, and qigong classes out there, but if you don't have the time (or money), simply look classes up online. There are many free classes on the internet that will help you learn the basics of these eastern healing practices.
- **Reiki.** Reiki is another alternative healing practice that originated in Japan. By learning reiki or seeking out a reiki practitioner, you will provide yourself with another powerful grounding option. Reiki is the practice of accessing universal source energy and channeling that energy through the hands and into the body.
- **Mindfulness.** Mindfulness is about paying attention to the present moment and grounding yourself through your senses. What can you see, hear, smell, taste, and feel around you? When you bring your awareness to these sensations, you will immediately become grounded.
- **Meditation.** Meditation is the practice of calming the mind and creating inner stillness. Almost every spiritual tradition, in some way, utilizes meditation as a way of connecting with one's Higher Self. Numerous studies have shown that meditation is the ideal way to lower anxiety, increase memory, enhance energy, and even decrease depression. Try experimenting with ten

minutes of meditation a day, then increase the time once you are more comfortable with the practice.

- **Art Therapy.** Creative expression is a powerful way to ground yourself and release the energy of other people that you may be carrying. In fact, art therapy can actually be a form of meditation when done in a calm space. Think of ways that you can creatively express yourself: do you enjoy painting, sculpting, drawing, crafting or some other form of art?

- **Deep Breathing.** Instead of breathing shallowly, try to deepen your breath and breathe through your belly. Not only does deep breathing infuse your body with more oxygen and energy, but it also helps to reduce stress and ground you in the moment.

These are just some of the many techniques out there which are particularly helpful for empaths. Some of these techniques such as mindfulness and deep breathing can be practiced in any moment or situation for on-the-spot grounding.

Practice 3 – Body Scan Meditation

The body scan meditation is a form of Vipassana meditation that draws awareness to different parts of your body. As an empath, you have the tendency to store a lot of emotional tension within different areas of your physical body. The more emotionally congested you are, the more you will experience chronic pain issues in different parts of your body. This tendency to hold emotional energy within the body for too long is one of the main causes of constant health issues like fibromyalgia and chronic fatigue syndrome (CFS) that we tend to so commonly develop as empaths.

Emotions manifest as energy experienced throughout the body. When you bring mindful awareness to your body, you

166

can instantly locate where this emotional energy is being stored. The moment you can pinpoint where any toxic energy is stored within your body is the moment you can release it by consciously relaxing.

The best thing about the body scan meditation is that it can be done in a very short period of time, and in virtually any moment. All you need to do is connect with your breath and draw attention to your body. However, for the best impact, I recommend that you try this practice in the comfort of your own house in a quiet space. The body scan meditation requires you to focus, and this can sometimes take a bit of practice.

If you're an empath who struggles with chronic health issues, particularly pain-related illnesses, you will find the body scan meditation particularly effective.

Here is how to get started with a five minute body scan:

1. Sit or lie down. Focus on your breath, and allow it to naturally deepen so that your stomach is gently rising and falling.
2. Once you are anchored in the present moment with your breath, bring awareness to your feet and ankles. Become curious: what sensations are in your feet? Do they feel cold, warm, soft, hard, numb, stiff, achy, heavy or any other sensation? Allow your breath to gently relax your feet and any sensations you feel. Don't worry if your feet don't feel completely relaxed; you can always return to them later.
3. Next, bring your awareness to your legs. Be curious and explore the sensations you feel. What word defines how you feel in your legs? Breathe into your legs and allow them to gently relax.

4. Next, bring your awareness to your hips. What physical sensations are stored in your hips? Allow your focus to be open and non-judgmental. Simply continue anchoring yourself in the present moment with your breath, and breathe into your hips. Try breathing five or more times gently into your hips until you're ready to move on.

5. Next, move on to your torso. How do your back and stomach feel? Focus on one sensation at a time if you have a lot of pain in this region. For example, if your back is sore and your stomach is stiff, focus on your back first. Allow your breath to subtly relax the muscles in your back. Then, focus on your stomach. With non-judgmental curiosity, pay attention to whatever feelings arise. Breathe deeply into the pain and relax.

6. After that, move on to your arms and hands. In what precise places do you feel tension, numbness, heaviness, stiffness, or any other sensation? Breathe into these sensations, allowing them to expand and soften.

7. Next, focus on your shoulders. Can you feel any tension, soreness or heaviness? Breathe, and relax.

8. Next, focus on your neck. Curiously explore the feelings within this region. Allow your deep breath to expand and relax these feelings.

9. Afterwards, bring awareness to your face and head. Allow your eyebrows, mouth, jaw, and any other muscles to relax. Use your breath and feel these regions rest.

10. Return to any other parts of your body that still feel tense or heavy. Bring your awareness gently to these regions, and continue breathing deeply.

11. Take some time to rest and relax after your body scan is complete.

What happens when, for example, you come across a person who is transmitting intensely heavy and negative energy? For on-the-spot relaxation, try connecting to your breath, allowing your breath to deepen, and paying attention to where tension in your body arises. By using your awareness and breath, you can unwind any parts of yourself that are starting to tense up or become heavy with emotional energy.

As a highly energy-sensitive person, you may even like to adopt the body scan as your formal meditation practice!

Practice 4 – Herbs

Herbs are a gentle but powerful way to increase your general health and wellbeing as an empath. If you're struggling with problems such as anxiety, irritability, insomnia, depression, and an overactive nervous system, there are so many empath-friendly herbs out there which can help you.

Herbs have been used since the dawn of humanity to cure numerous ailments. If you're like most empaths, conventional medicines tend to make you feel worse as they're not suited to your delicate nervous system. Herbs, on the other hand, are generally non-invasive but effective ways to remedy physical and even emotional problems. While taking medications is, in some circumstances, vital, it is not always imperative that we go to the chemist to buy drugs that will make us feel better. Herbs are a healthy alternative.

For example, many years ago I was prescribed Prozac for the anxiety I experienced. The only problem was that when I took this drug, I felt completely numbed out and depressed – like many empaths who are prescribed pharmaceutical drugs. The moment I stopped taking Prozac and instead started taking damiana leaf (which is a native American shrub), I finally felt like myself again, minus the tense nerves.

Here are some of the best herbs for empaths out there based on our most common needs: anxiety and stress reduction, hormone regulation, depression reduction, and energy preservation.

Holy Basil – Holy Basil is an adaptogen that helps the body adapt to stress. It has a sweet, slightly peppery taste and is a very effective herb for balancing the energy field.

Rhodiola Rosea – Rhodiola increases the body's resistance to stress by regulating its hormones and improving neurotransmitter activity within the brain towards anxiety. Rhodiola is also said to help reduce depression, fatigue, cholesterol, altitude sickness, and other physical and mental ailments.

Ashwagandha – Ashwagandha is traditionally used in Ayurvedic medicine and has been shown to reduce anxiety as well as enhance libido, decrease blood pressure, soothe ADHD, reduce arthritic swelling, and help with many other bodily afflictions.

Maca Root – Maca is considered a superfood that boosts your energy, increases fertility, and balances hormones.

Yerba Mate – Yerba Mate is a great alternative to coffee for empaths because it has similar energy-boosting effects, but with rarely any side effects.

Damiana – Damiana is a wonderfully potent herb for psychological stress. It is also an aphrodisiac, and can even help reduce depression.

Ginkgo Biloba – Ginkgo Biloba naturally enhances your energy and mental concentration by improving blood circulation and lowering oxidative stress in the body. Ginkgo also helps soothe PMS; helps to treat ADHD; heals headaches, migraines, and tinnitus; and is used by those with fibromyalgia to soothe the nervous system. Ginkgo is also well known for its ability to reduce anxiety and depression.

Siberian Ginseng – Siberian Ginseng helps the body adapt to a variety of physical and mental stresses such as insomnia, too much work, chronic anxiety, and immunity impairment.

Raw Cacao – Raw Cacao has a truly stunning array of benefits. Cacao not only increases energy, but it is also a natural antidepressant as it boosts the "happy chemicals" in your brain. Cacao lowers blood pressure, protects the nervous system, lowers insulin resistance, guards your body against toxins, and reduces your risks of cardiovascular disease. A little bit of raw cacao goes a long way, so try a tiny amount first!

Passionflower – Passionflower boosts overall mood and mental health. It also helps to reduce insomnia, anxiety, and ADHD.

Valerian – Valerian is most commonly used for insomnia as it heavily relaxes the body. Only take Valerian at night before bed, as it tends to make you very sleepy.

You may also like to explore Kava Kava, Lemon Balm, Skull Cap, and St. John's Wort. As with any herb, make sure you check if they interact negatively with any medications you may be taking. Also, some of these herbs don't suit pregnant women, so if you're with child, research first.

The best thing is that many of these herbs can easily be grown in your own backyard. Alternatively, you can easily find most of these herbs in your local health food shop or online herb distributor.

Practice 5 – Aromatherapy

Essential oils are a particularly effective and exhilarating way of soothing, purifying, and even energizing your body. When we inhale essential oils, the molecules travel through the nose and stimulate the limbic system within our brains – also known as the "emotional brain." In this sense, essential oils are particularly good at grounding and stabilizing the mind-body connection.

The physiological and psychological effects that essential oils can have on us as empaths is profound. Below, I will share with you some of the best suited essential oils for empaths, divided into our five different requirements.

Grounding

- Rosemary
- Patchouli
- Sandalwood
- Oakmoss
- Cypress
- Rosewood
- Cedarwood
- Pine
- Juniper
- Bay Laurel

Lowering Anxiety

- Lavender
- Rose
- Clary Sage
- Neroli
- Bergamot
- Basil

- Frankincense
- Ylang Ylang

Strengthening Your Energy Field

- Sage
- Patchouli
- Frankincense
- Myrrh
- Peppermint
- Sandalwood
- Rosemary
- Tea Tree
- Eucalyptus

Promoting Self-Love and Healthy Boundaries

- Rose
- Geranium
- Bergamot
- Clary Sage
- Jasmine
- Neroli
- Patchouli
- Orange
- Frankincense
- Cedarwood
- Rosewood

Lowering Fatigue and Increasing Energy

- Lemon
- Basil
- Cinnamon

- Orange
- Grapefruit
- Spearmint
- Rosemary
- Pine
- Black Pepper
- Ginger
- Eucalyptus

The wonderful thing about essential oils is that they can be made into tinctures, salves, and diffused around your work and home environment. You might also like to try using these essential oils in a warm bath, in a compress for your muscles or simply applied topically to your skin. Remember, a few of these oils require dilution with carrier oils (such as coconut oil) before you apply them to your skin, so ensure you research further. Even simply giving a whiff of these essential oils right out of the bottle will quickly benefit your body.

Practice 6 – Crystals

For thousands of years crystals have been used in spiritual practice and healing processes. The use of crystals dates all the way back 6,000 years ago to the ancient Sumerians in Mesopotamia. Since then, crystals have been used in one form or another in countless ancient cultures such as in Egypt, China, Rome, Greece, and South America.

Metaphysically, crystals vibrate at their own frequencies, just like everything that is composed of energy. When introduced to our own energy fields, crystals create larger vibrational fields and affect our nervous systems through the Law of Resonance. These shifting vibrations can help to stimulate a number of mind-body forms of healing.

There are many crystals out there which are perfectly suited to empaths. Below I will share with you some of the most ideal ones for our needs:

Shungite – Shungite is an ancient stone only found in Russia that is around two billion years old. The energy of shungite is astounding and extremely powerful, and almost anyone who handles this stone will feel its vibration. That being said, shungite is not for every empath. I know of some empaths that find this stone simply too overwhelming, and others who find it extremely grounding and stabilizing. Shungite is a powerful stone for purifying toxic and repressed energy stored within your body. It is often referred to as a "protection stone." Use this stone when you need fierce support, cleansing, empowerment, and grounding. Shungite has even been scientifically proven to purify water.[3] I wear a piece of shungite close to my heart every day.

Blue Kyanite – Blue kyanite is another one of those dynamic, high vibration crystals. Use it to help release emotional blocks, transform and ground energy, elevate your consciousness, and help you access your inner truth.

Rose Quartz – Rose quartz is a gentle stone that is often associated with unconditional love. Use rose quartz to help you access self-love, express buried emotions, promote forgiveness, and transmute pain into love.

Black Tourmaline – Black tourmaline is an ideal grounding crystal for all empaths. Use this stone to cleanse, transform, and purify negative energy. Black tourmaline is also said to help remove blockages within the energy field or aura.

Lepidolite – Lepidolite is ideal for anxiety-ridden empaths. Use this stone for reducing stress, panic, and fear. Lepidolite is also helpful in soothing mind-body related illnesses related to tense nervous systems (such as chronic fatigue).

Rhodonite – Rhodonite is a stone of the heart. Use rhodonite when you need to protect and nurture your own emotional energy. Rhodonite helps you to also increase unconditional love towards yourself and others.

Carnelian – Carnelian is a vibrant stone of self-empowerment. Use carnelian whenever you need to access more inner energy, strength, and confidence. Carnelian is particularly useful if you struggle to set boundaries around pushy people and energy vampires.

Tiger's Eye – Tiger's eye is a stone of strength and clarity. Use tiger's eye when you need to set clear boundaries and understand issues in your life with keen perception. Tiger's eye can help you to identify people who are not good for your health.

Yellow Jasper – Yellow jasper is primarily associated with protection. Use yellow jasper to calm and ground your emotions, increase self-esteem, and unify different aspects of your life.

Moonstone – Moonstone is a powerful stone for emotional mastery. Use moonstone to help you access and release the emotional energy you absorb. Moonstone will help you to release emotions stored in your unconscious mind and cleanse your energy field.

Hematite – Hematite is a wonderful stone for grounding and balancing energy. Use hematite during stressful periods to help you access your inner calmness and strength. Hematite is said to help stimulate blood flow in the body which increases mental clarity and helps to release energetic toxins.

Purple Jade – Purple jade is a stone of discernment. Use purple jade to help you distinguish your energy from other people's energy. Purple jade will help you to access mental and spiritual clarity, while simultaneously grounding you.

Please note that none of these stones should be used as a replacement for professional therapeutic support. Instead, think of these crystals as helpers and supporters of your growth as an empath.

The best way to make use of crystals is by wearing them close to your body or meditating with them. Many crystal healing practitioners recommend cleansing your crystals every now and then to reset their vibrational field. Cleansing can be done by smudging, running the crystals under water, putting them in the sunlight or moonlight, burying them in the earth, or using sound vibration such as a singing bowl or tuning fork.

Practice 6 – Grounding Food

All food is energy, and as empaths, certain types of food suit us better than others. Whatever we put into our bodies directly influences our capacity to stay relaxed, grounded, perceptive, and conscious. Therefore, it makes sense to choose the food we eat carefully and considerately as empaths. After all, our bodies are the vessels in which we inhabit, and when our bodies are impaired, we are psychologically and emotionally impaired.

The idea of grounding foods originates from Chinese medicine and its theory that each food carries a certain vibration. The unique vibration of each source of food we eat is thought to influence every aspect of our being; from our physical energy levels, to mood and even mental health. A slaughtered cow for example will have a much different vibration from an organic garden salad. And the notion that food directly influences our mental and emotional states isn't just a hypothesis. Numerous studies have proven the modern truism that "you are what you eat." For example, in a paper released in 2008, professor of neurosurgery and physiological science Fernando Gómez-Pinilla analyzed more than 160 studies about food's effect on the brain. Gómez-Pinilla discovered that certain foods actually increase or decrease our chances of developing issues such as depression, various mood disorders, schizophrenia, and dementia.[4] Junk food (processed food), for example, is a notorious example of food that triggers physical and mental illnesses. As empaths, we would do well to cut out as many processed foods as possible, and eat more food that will help to nourish and ground us. If you're like most empaths, you probably also have a delicate nervous system. If you're struggling with issues such as anxiety, you might also like to try and reduce your intake of sugar and caffeine. Stimulants are designed to put an intense strain on the nervous system. For highly sensitive types, this strain tends to create more long-term harm than good.

Drawing on the principles of Chinese medicine and modern scientific discovery, here is a list of some of the best grounding foods to eat as an empath:

Fruit

- Apricot
- Avocado
- Cherries
- Coconut
- Dates
- Figs
- Guava
- Kumquat
- Longan
- Lychee
- Mango
- Nectarines
- Papaya
- Peach
- Pineapple
- Plum
- Raspberry

Vegetables

- Asparagus
- Beetroot
- Broccoli
- Carrot
- Chinese cabbage
- Corn
- Daikon
- Eggplant
- Leek
- Olives
- Onion
- Parsnip
- Peppers (Capsicum)
- Potato

- Pumpkin
- Radish
- Rutabaga (Swede)
- Sea vegetables such as wakame and nori
- Spinach
- Squash
- Sweet Potato
- Tomato
- Turnip

Grains

- Amaranth
- Barley
- Buckwheat
- Lentils
- Millet
- Oats
- Quinoa
- Rice (brown, white, wild)
- Rye
- Wheat

Legumes & Nuts

- Adzuki bean
- Almond
- Black bean
- Broad bean
- Chestnut
- Kidney bean
- Peanut
- Pinenut
- Pistachio

- Soybean
- Walnut

Meat and Dairy

While meat and dairy are very grounding, they also tend to be full of hormones and intensely negative energetic residue from the animals involved. Try to reduce your intake of meat and dairy as much as you can. You might even like to change to vegetarian or vegan eating as an ethical alternative. Many empaths are vegans or vegetarians. If you must eat meat and dairy, ensure that you buy organic, grass fed, sustainable, and preferably locally sourced.

- Cheese
- Eggs
- Pork
- Poultry
- Red meat
- Seafood

Miscellaneous

- Brown sugar
- Coconut sugar
- Pumpkin, sunflower, and sesame seeds
- Rapeseed oil
- Sea salt
- Sesame oil
- Soy beans
- Soy sauce
- Sunflower oil

You may also like to use the following spices more often:

- Anise
- Basil
- Chives
- Cinnamon
- Cloves
- Cumin
- Dill
- Fennel
- Garlic
- Ginger
- Ginseng
- Nutmeg
- Rosemary
- Tarragon

Most of these foods possess yang energy according to Chinese medicine, which is the type of warm and strong energy we need as empaths. The opposite of yang energy is yin energy, which is cold and passive energy (which we need less of).

Remember that your body is unique and only *you* can truly know what feels right. Try experimenting with the fruits, vegetables, and other food types mentioned in this chapter. Explore which foods enhance your energy, which foods are too heavy, and which foods seem to disrupt your inner balance. For example, my favorite grounding foods are pumpkin, sweet potato, cinnamon, brown rice, ginger, and coconut. But my body seems to reject wheat, peanuts, pineapple, dates, and soybean. Find what works for you!

Practice 7 – Create a Renewal Zone

We live in an age that constantly demands us to be switched on. Each day, we face numerous sources of energy exhaustion, whether they be working in a busy job, catering to others' needs, taking care of children, keeping the household in order, or juggling all of these at once. Life for us empaths can get pretty draining and daunting very quickly. Sooner or later, we start getting seriously ill, especially when we neglect to set aside small chunks of the day to recharge our energy. Unfortunately, the only period of "downtime" we usually get occurs at night when we collapse onto the couch or into our beds, after the day's work. Even then, many of us struggle to sleep due to our overactive nervous systems, making daily life truly draining and debilitating.

What can we do to prevent ourselves from burning out? One of the best practices is to create renewal zones during the day. Renewal zones honor the ebb and flow of our energy, and allow us to regularly access moments of energetic grounding and rejuvenation.

As an empath, it is vital that you create numerous renewal zones, or sacred spaces, during the day. As a general rule, try to create three or more regular periods in your day to take a break. These renewal periods must be held as sacred and unbreakable. In other words, they should be seen as vital to your well-being, and should therefore be strategically picked.

There are two kinds of renewal zones. The first is the static renewal zone which is a physical place that is dedicated to relaxing and recentering. For example, you might choose a room of your house, a bench outside or corner of your workplace as a renewal zone. The second is the ritualized renewal zone. Sometimes it's not possible for us to choose static renewal zones due to the nature of our work (for example, if our job requires us to move around a lot). Ritualized renewal zones are basically rituals that we create which help us to disconnect from the demands of daily life. The best thing about rituals is that we can usually do them in almost any moment, no matter where we are. Examples of ritualized renewal zones include taking five minutes to listen to calming music, going outside and breathing in fresh air, spending time practicing a form of relaxation (like the body scan), doodling in an art journal, or any number of other practices.

Creating your own renewal zones is about taking back control of your life. Society teaches us to ignore our own ebb and flow of energy – but you don't need to let your needs be devalued or ignored any longer. It's time to step up and reclaim your need to rest! After all, it is completely unnatural to be constantly "on the job" all day. Like any other being on this planet, you need space to just be, without the need to do.

The following tips will help you identify, pick, and establish the best renewal zones for you throughout the day:

1. Identify tiring periods of your day.

Renewal zones work the best when they coincide with our energy slumps. Choose the most tiring periods of your day and assign renewal zones to them. Alternatively, you can choose periods when you need the most grounding. For example, you might like to start off your mornings by establishing a renewal zone or after attending business meetings. Try to identify a minimum of three periods.

2. Designate a renewal place or ritual.

Once you've identified three tiring periods of your day, choose a physical place or ritual that will help you relax and regenerate energy. Remember, renewal zones are highly personal and contextual. Some days you might feel like taking a fifteen minute nap, while on other days you might feel like sipping a warm cup of tea slowly outside. Sometimes you may not have a lot of privacy, so you might choose to simply focus on your breath instead.

Here are a few examples of renewal zones and rituals you can use:

- Meditation
- Going outside and breathing in fresh air
- Watching nature
- Making and drinking tea
- Practicing mindfulness
- Listening to music
- Tuning into your breath
- Taking a short power nap
- Closing your eyes
- Spending time alone
- Drawing
- Doing yoga
- Making artwork
- Sitting outside
- Sitting in a quiet room or space (even the toilet cubicle will do!)
- Watch a funny video
- Repeating a mantra or affirmation
- Stretching

These are just a few of many possibilities. Get creative! Just try to resist the temptation to fill your renewal space with more "doing" or productivity. The whole point is to do as little as possible!

3. Assign a chunk of time.

How long will you spend in your renewal zone? While your needs will change every day, it does help to approach your renewal time with an idea of how much time you plan on relaxing. The more mentally organized you are, the more you will benefit from these renewal periods without worrying about your other duties. Ask yourself, "How much time can I spare?" Once you have mentally assigned a period of time such as five minutes or even half an hour, you will be able to easily incorporate these renewal periods throughout your day.

Remember, your renewal zones are unique to you and your empathic needs. As such, they should be something you look forward to and try to actively introduce into your schedule! Without creating sacred pockets within your day to intentionally "turn off," it can be near impossible to remain grounded as an empath. Even taking a couple of minutes to stop and breathe deeply in the midst of a frantic schedule will help you become more grounded and internally balanced. The more grounded you are, the better you can preserve your energy, create boundaries, and experience emotional freedom as an empath.

Chapter 15 – Healing the Mental Realm

"A thought is harmless until we believe it. It's not our thoughts but our attachment to our thoughts that causes suffering." – ***Byron Katie***

One of the best avenues for developing inner strength, wisdom, and wholeness as an empath is by exploring your mind. Your mind is like an intricate labyrinth that contains passage after passage of hidden memories, beliefs, ideals, and wounds that directly influence your relationship with yourself, others, and existence. When you become an explorer of these complex inner labyrinths, you uncover hidden doorways and even buried keys that help you to unlock the root of your overwhelming fears and dysfunctions.

In this chapter, I'll share with you five of the very best techniques and practical tools out there that you can use to journey into the labyrinths of your mind. These practices are frequently used in our work to help and empower highly sensitive empath clients who struggle with problems such as chronic fatigue, anxiety disorders, toxic relationships, and low self-esteem.

As you progress through this chapter, you'll notice that each practice is separated into different sections like the last chapter. As there is a lot of rich and highly applicable information in this chapter, you'll benefit from stopping and pausing after each section, and reflecting on how you can implement the strategies recommended into your life.

Practice 1 – Exploring Mistaken Beliefs

It is no secret that our thoughts influence our reality. While we're predominantly feeling-centered people, it's also important that we examine the role our minds play in our daily lives as empaths. Without examining our thoughts, we can easily fall into patterns of self-sabotaging behavior, sometimes without even knowing it.

Mistaken beliefs are thoughts that we have been either conditioned to believe from our parents, teachers, or society, or distorted perceptions we have adopted from repeated life experiences. When mistaken beliefs go unnoticed and function beneath the level of our conscious awareness, they quickly end up running our lives. Inevitably, rogue mistaken beliefs cause many of the shadow issues we experience as empaths such as self-victimization, chronic fears and illnesses, energetic burnout, and depleting relationships.

A mistaken belief cannot be supported by facts or logic. Some of the most commonly held mistaken beliefs that empaths carry include:

- I am responsible for other people's happiness.
- I am responsible for other people's healing.
- I should always be available to those I love.
- I should always put other people first.
- I should always take care of everyone.
- If I spend time taking care of myself before others, that makes me selfish.
- I should never get angry or hurt.
- I should always be open and happy.
- I should always be generous.
- My feelings and needs are unimportant.

188

- People won't like me if I don't take care of them.
- I'm powerless.
- I am a victim of outside circumstances.
- My gifts make me a victim of life.
- My condition is hopeless.
- There is something fundamentally wrong with me.
- If a person I love doesn't love me in return, it's my fault.
- Life is a struggle.
- I should be the perfect friend/partner/parent/son/daughter.
- The world is always a dangerous place.
- My self-worth has to be earned.
- My problems will go away on their own in time.
- I am controlled by other people's energy.
- I always know what other people are feeling and thinking.

The problem with mistaken beliefs is that they are often so fundamental to our perception of life that we don't recognize them. The less conscious we are of our mistaken beliefs, the more constricting they become and the more they tend to evolve into self-fulfilling prophecies. In other words, if I believe that my feelings and needs are not important, I will behave in ways that reflect this belief and attract people into my life who will confirm it. Similarly, if you believe that you must always put other people first, you will carry that belief out and accustom people to taking advantage of your self-sacrificing actions so that they are constantly expecting more from you.

Not only can mistaken beliefs become self-fulfilling prophecies, but they also keep us locked in cages of fear, insecurity, and disempowerment. These cages restrict our ability to experience personal fulfillment, wellbeing, and the achievement of our ultimate life purpose. But we usually aren't

189

aware of these cages. We aren't aware because we are so habituated to the false sense of safety and security that these mistaken beliefs provide us with. As a result, we tend to become protective of our beliefs, because without them, we feel naked, vulnerable, and exposed. So if you found yourself having a surprising emotional reaction while reading the list above, don't worry. It can be threatening to challenge your beliefs. But it can also be liberating.

The only way to become liberated from your mistaken beliefs is by first identifying them. So make sure you take the time to go through the list above and highlight or write down any of the mistaken beliefs you can identify with. Feel free to also create your own. Just *recognizing* your mistaken beliefs is an amazingly important step toward letting them go.

After you've recognized and identified your mistaken beliefs, you can then start the process of deconstructing them. We'll explore how to disassemble mistaken beliefs soon.

Practice 2 – Exploring Core Beliefs

Our core beliefs, while similar to mistaken beliefs, are much more central to who we believe we are deep down. As empaths, it's essential that we make the unconscious within us conscious; in other words, it's essential that we learn how to uncover the hidden beliefs we have that influence our waking reality. Our capacity to energetically connect with and support others while maintaining a balanced and healthy inner self is highly dependent on the core beliefs we carry about ourselves.

When our core beliefs are positive and supportive, we're able to allow the emotional and mental energy of others to pass through us, while staying grounded. On the other hand, when our core beliefs are negative and unsupportive, we tend to absorb the emotions of others like sponges and carry them within our bodies and energy fields. These "secondhand" emotions, in turn, create huge amounts of emotional turbulence within us, which can lead to serious health problems.

Like mistaken beliefs, core beliefs were inherited from our parents, societies, teachers, and religious institutions. The difference is that core beliefs are the fundamental convictions we have about ourselves; they are the absolute truths we have developed about ourselves throughout the course of our entire lives. Core beliefs underlie a large percentage of the thoughts, beliefs, emotions, choices, and preferences we have. Everything from the partners we choose, to the jobs we keep, to the daily decisions we make are based on the core beliefs we have.

Core beliefs represent the mother of all our beliefs and they are often the root cause of our suffering. In fact, uncovering core beliefs is a central practice I often recommend to my clients because of how intensely life-transforming the practice can be.

But here's a word of caution: not everyone is prepared to fully meet their core beliefs, because it requires absolute honesty and vulnerability. When I share the common list of core beliefs with my clients, I'm often met with resistance in the form of disbelief or skepticism, along the lines of, "I can't believe that I'd think that, it sounds so silly."

The reality is that, yes, core beliefs can sound silly because they are fundamentally misguided ideas about ourselves. But that doesn't make them any less real.

Below, read through the common list of core beliefs and pay attention to any feelings that arise while reading them. The feelings you may or may not receive are a good indication of which core beliefs are closest to those you hold:

I am unlikeable.
I am unlovable.
I am irredeemably flawed.
I am bad.
I am stupid.
I am worthless.
I am a loser.
I don't deserve good things.
I am unworthy of happiness.
I am a failure.
I am weak.
I am not enough.
I don't matter.
I am boring.
I am crazy and unstable.
I can't be fixed.
I always hurt people.
I always hurt myself.
I have no hope.
I am evil/sinful.
I deserve to be punished.
I am unwanted.
I am invisible.
I am a mistake.
I am helpless.
I am powerless.
I am ugly.
I am shameful.

I will die alone.

As you can see, core beliefs always start with an "I ..." statement, and they are exclusively related to self-worth.

As Cindy, a client of mine, related to me, "My belief that I was an unstable person was actually screwing up all of my working and personal relationships to the point that I was becoming the very thing I feared the most. Now that I know this is just a false belief I've given myself the freedom to see everything with new eyes, including the serial gaslighters who were using my fear of being unstable against me. Discovering this core belief literally changed my life so that now I can love the true me instead of the 'me' through distorted thoughts."

Practice 3 – Journaling

One of the best ways to expose your mistaken beliefs and core beliefs is through regular journaling. Journaling, both formally and informally, is a deceptively simple but remarkably powerful way of accessing your innermost thoughts, feelings, and beliefs. I like to think of journaling as a conversation between your ego and your Soul. Your ego is the socially constructed part of you that is formed from your feelings, beliefs, ideals, desires, thoughts, memories, and preferences. Your Soul, on the other hand, is that eternal and unchanging part within you that is fundamentally who you are at your core. While the ego is subject to change, the Soul is timeless, wise, and ever-present.

When we journal, we record all of our thoughts and feelings in a notebook or word document as a form of self-reflection. The part of us that observes and understands the meaning of our thoughts and feelings, as well as sends us intuitive signals, is our Soul.

Journaling needs to be undertaken daily for it to make a real difference in your life. Don't worry, you don't need to be a writer or even particularly good at spelling to record your thoughts. The most important thing is that you have a record of your feelings and perspectives so you can reflect on them later.

When first starting journaling, I always recommend that people write whatever comes to mind, or whatever happened that day. The point of journaling isn't to get philosophical, but to write down exactly what you think and feel in an unfiltered fashion. If you feel the need to write in caps lock or capital letters to express your anger, go for it. If you feel the need to swear or say obscene things, even better! Journaling is a tool of self-expression and even emotional catharsis. It's a safe way for you to release any suppressed feelings you've been having, and a healthy way to explore your thinking patterns.

Here's an example from one of my clients who courageously chose to be vulnerable and share his feelings with me from his journal:

"I hate going to work. I'm really hating it. I hate the energy there, I hate having to talk with stupid fucking people all the time. Arghhhhh ... I guess I'm just feeling tired and sad today. This job is not fulfilling me and not what I expected. Every time I come home I feel exhausted, and then I have to put on a happy face for the kids. I feel undervalued and like my life is going nowhere. People dump their crap onto me all the time, and I just want to tell them to STOP. But it makes me feel bad

194

– yeah, of *course* I'd feel that way. I'm just too sensitive. So I don't know what to do or where to go. I just feel trapped."

It's important that you say everything that's on your mind and in your heart when you're journaling. People often make the mistake of trying to make what they write nice or somehow "spiritualizing" their words, but this is just hiding behind another mask. The purpose of journaling is to be your most raw, authentic self, in a completely uncensored way. Journaling is about pulling down all the facades and roles and writing the truth of how you feel. In order to write truthfully, you need to give yourself the permission to be a bit messy, loud, and even "damaged."

When you can write in an uncensored way and get out all of your pent-up thoughts and feelings, you can then practice reflecting on your words from a quieter place. This quiet place is the non-judgmental, open, curious, and perceptive space within your Soul. Through time, you will notice patterns of thoughts and feelings emerging. For example, you might notice that you frequently feel angry and taken for granted around your friends, or you might carry certain mistaken beliefs about who you are as a person. Eventually, you'll be able to pinpoint the precise beliefs you carry, what triggers certain negative emotions within you, and destructive behavioral patterns in your life.

As an empath, you will greatly benefit from journaling. The more you're capable of introspection and self-awareness (which are skills developed by journaling), the more you'll be aware of the internal and external factors that cause you to feel weighed down with emotion. In other words, you'll be able to distinguish between *your* emotions and *other people's* emotions. This skill is absolutely essential as an empath.

Some useful questions that will help get you started with journaling include the following:

- What am I feeling today?
- Why do I feel or think these thoughts?
- When did I begin thinking these feelings and thoughts?
- What situations triggered negative emotions in me today or this week?
- What situations inspired happiness within me this week?
- What situations did I feel fatigued in and why?
- What situations did I feel energized in and why?
- What patterns can I notice emerge in my emotions and thoughts?
- What people or places seem to have a toxic effect on me?
- What people or places cause me to feel loved and supported
- What words do I wish I could say to someone?

If you've not had much experience journaling before, I recommend just sticking with the first question, "What am I feeling today?" and then slowly building from there.

Through time, you can read back on your journal entries and highlight any negative phrases or feelings that seem to repeat over and over again. If you struggle to find repetitive thoughts or feelings, simply highlight any painful adjectives or phrases. For example, you might choose to highlight words and phrases such as "sick in my stomach," "misunderstood," "I am sacrificing too much," "unheard," "no time to rest," "angry," "I always have to do everything," and so forth. The more you highlight, the more you will notice emotional and mental patterns arising. However, I recommend that you only reflect on and highlight your journal once a week, otherwise, you will become distracted from the process of writing.

Once you are aware of the emotional and mental thought patterns that arise in you, you can question them by simply asking "why?"

From your journal, choose a few thoughts, and next to each thought ask "why?" or the questions, "Why is that so bad/Why is that so important?" Keep asking these questions until you reach a core answer. For example, you might choose the thought, "I hate how my friend keeps interrupting me." Why is that so bad? "Because I want to be listened to." Why? "Because I want to be cared for." Why? "Because I feel like no one cares about what I have to say." Why is that so important? "Because I feel alone and worthless." From this we can ascertain that the core beliefs would be, "I am worthless" or "I am alone."

Practice 4 – Honest Affirmations

Once you have identified your mistaken or core beliefs, you can begin deprogramming yourself through the creation of honest affirmations. The reason why I have written "honest" affirmations is that many people approach affirmations from an ingenuine mindset. The purpose of creating affirmations isn't to fool yourself into believing something you secretly don't believe is true about yourself, but is instead about creating a statement your heart and Soul honestly resonates with.

When creating affirmations, you should aim to keep them short, simple, and direct. You'll benefit from keeping them in the present tense (e.g. "I am strong" instead of "I am becoming

197

a strong person") so that they have maximum impact. It's also important that you avoid negatively phrased affirmations. For example, instead of saying "I'm not a fatigued person," say, "I am full of vibrancy and energy."

In order to work with honest affirmations, you need to choose a few issues in your life that cause you emotional distress. As an empath, this could be anything from your tendency to have poor boundaries, to your habit of overextending yourself in service of others. If you're struggling to identify a specific issue, read and reflect on your journal.

Once you have picked an issue, write it down on a piece of paper or word document. For example, you might write, "I feel overwhelmed by other people." Next to this statement, write an affirmation that feels more honest and empowering to you as a reflection of your true self. For instance, you might write, "I set strong and stable boundaries around others." Or perhaps you struggle with putting everyone before yourself. You might write as an affirmation, "I am learning to love myself." If you're struggling to create present tense affirmations because they sound too strong, you can always try phrasing them in future tense, e.g. if saying "I am confident" sounds incorrect to you, say "I am gaining confidence every day."

Here are some sample affirmations that may help you reprogram negative beliefs as an empath:

- It's OK for me to take time to rest and relax.
- I am learning to be assertive every day.
- I am strong and courageous.
- I respect my needs and desires.
- I let go of pain effortlessly.
- I am raising my vibration.

- I am inherently worthy.
- I am responsible for my happiness.
- I let go of all energy that is not mine.
- I have a strong energy field.
- I am resilient in the face of suffering.
- My heart is full of love for life and other people.
- I let go and let love show me the way.
- I witness the energy within me and allow it to pass through me.
- All the power I need to create a fulfilling life is within me.
- I release all emotions and thoughts that no longer serve me.
- My heart is open and I welcome all energy to pass through without affecting me.
- I create strong and clear boundaries.
- I respect my boundaries.
- I flow with life.
- I allow all emotions within me to be transformed for my highest good.
- I am divinely guided.
- I love the person I am.
- I am kind and discerning.
- I am sensitive and powerful.
- I give myself the freedom to walk away from others.
- I allow my Soul's wisdom to lead the way.
- I am learning how to become a balanced person.
- I honor my limitations.
- My inner strength amazes me.
- I am open to life.

These are just a few of the many possible affirmations out there you can create as an empath. You're welcome to choose one from this list, or write one yourself.

After you have chosen one or two affirmations that speak to you, your job is to incorporate them into your daily life. The more you repeat your affirmations to yourself and the deeper you come to believe them, the more quickly your mental blockages become cleared. You can repeat your affirmation as a mantra during meditation or throughout the day, write it on a note that you keep in your wallet, repeat it in your journal every day, or post it around your house. Whatever you choose, ensure that you repeatedly read your affirmation every day. Continue this practice for a month and reflect on how it influences you. Through time, your affirmation will reprogram your thinking patterns so that you no longer struggle with limiting mistaken and core beliefs about yourself and others.

Practice 5 – Socratic Questioning

If you're not convinced by affirmations, you might like to explore socratic questioning instead. In fact, I recommend using both affirmations *and* socratic questioning on your healing journey. Socratic questioning is a tool that improves our critical thinking skills and helps us to be more objective as empaths. Let's face it, we could all do with being a little more objective about our perspectives and feelings. As empaths, we're particularly prone to getting confused and overwhelmed by other people's energy, so we're often in desperate need of finding some grounding.

Originating from the ancient Greek philosopher Socrates, socratic questioning uses pointed questions to help us reach the truth of any situation. In modern times, socratic questioning is continually used in professions such as teaching, psychology, science, and even among spiritual guides such as self-inquiry teacher Byron Katie.

Five useful socratic questions include the following:

1. What is the evidence for this belief?
2. What is the evidence against this belief?
3. Do I know that this thought is 100% true? Why? (Or, is this *always* true for me?)
4. Did I choose this belief or did it develop from my childhood?
5. How would I feel without this belief?

These five questions can easily be applied to any mistaken or core belief you come across. Not only that, but you can actually teach yourself to ask any of these five questions in real life situations, making your perspective more emotionally and psychologically balanced.

In order to become a mature, balanced, and healed empath, you need to balance heart intelligence with the head intelligence. Socratic questioning is the perfect logical tool to use if you have a heart-head imbalance. All you need to do is choose one of your beliefs, and question it. You can do this mentally or on paper. I recommend having a visual representation of this process on paper first in order to get you used to questioning your thoughts.

As I mentioned in the shadow self chapter, we empaths struggle with a number of problems such as blame, projection, introjection, self-victimization, and low self-worth. Many of these issues stem from our mistaken and core beliefs. And our lack of energetic boundaries is only really a product of beliefs we've been taught throughout life. When we put our beliefs underneath the spotlight, we are actually helping ourselves to awaken as people.

There are so many benefits of practicing the socratic questioning method, including a sense of relief, renewed confidence, enhanced self-worth, and the wonderful feeling of liberation from limiting ideas.

Here's an example of how to apply socratic questioning:

1. Choose a thought or belief.

For example, you could choose a mistaken belief such as, "I am controlled by other people's emotions."

2. Apply the questioning.
Use each of the five questions (or whichever question you feel is relevant) to your belief. Here's an example:

What is the evidence for this belief?
After spending time with other people, I feel their toxic energy inside of me. I just seem to absorb it all like a sponge. I feel very unlike myself after being around lots of people, and that influences my behavior which makes me feel like I'm being controlled.

What is the evidence against this belief?
I don't always feel bad after spending time with people. It could be possible that I was feeling bad to begin with but didn't realize it. Maybe my hormones began acting up.

Do I know that this thought is 100% true? Why?
I don't one hundred percent know that I am controlled by other people's emotions, I only conclude that after spending time with people.

Did I choose this belief or did it develop from my childhood?
My mother was always blaming other people for the way she felt. So it could be possible that I adopted this belief from her as a way of explaining and disowning my suffering.

How would I feel without this belief?
I would feel more comfortable around people if I didn't believe their emotions are controlling me. I'd probably feel more relaxed and open around people as well, and more loving.

As we can see, socratic questioning can be very revealing. But this method requires absolute honesty and the openness and willingness to see that you might be misguided. For question three (*Do I know that this thought is 100% true? Why?*), for instance, you must be willing to deeply question your beliefs. It can be very easy to simply say, "yes, I do know this is true," and start running away into other mental stories and justifications. But do you absolutely know that your belief is true? Do you know every single thought, motivation and feeling, of others, and do you really know every possible scenario and the infinite array of possibilities out there? Unless you're an all-knowing being, I'm guessing your answer will be "no." Therefore, socratic questioning takes practice and radical honesty.

Once you manage to uncover, explore, and expose your mistaken and core beliefs through the methods described in this chapter, you can finally find mental freedom. Many people describe the feeling of releasing their core beliefs as the sensation of dropping unbearably heavy and burdensome baggage. I would personally describe the sensation of releasing core beliefs as being born again: the feeling of surrendering these old and toxic thought forms is incomparable. At last, you are free to become the person you're destined to become because you're no longer limited by false beliefs.

In order to make the most of our psychological healing journey, we need to be aware that it can take time. Please keep in mind that it's normal to feel frustrated, bored or even at times like we aren't making any progress whatsoever. But by making it our goal to dedicate ourselves to this growth no matter what, we gradually begin to experience deep internal changes that revolutionize the way we feel and think forever.

Chapter 16 – Healing the Emotional Realm

"I am 55, and have struggled with being an empath all of my life. I often think I am a lunatic. I can feel so much of other people ... it is very hard for people to fool me ... if they are pretending to be 'happy' but carry underlying pain, I feel it." – **Mona, empath reader from lonerwolf.com**

Emotional healing is fundamental to our healing journeys as empaths. Without identifying, distinguishing, understanding, and showing compassion for what we feel, we remain stranded in storms of chaotic and unpredictable emotions that can hijack our energy fields at any moment. However, when we learn how to stay grounded no matter what person or situation enters into our life, we can finally find inner harmony, peace, and joyous balance again. In other words, we can finally be our authentic and empowered selves once we learn how to deal with the emotional energy within us.

In this chapter, we'll explore how to deal with the foreign energy that you receive from other people and also the native emotional energy within you. The techniques and practices I will share have been used by both of us on our personal healing journeys as well as our students with immense success.

Like the last chapter, this chapter will also be broken down into bite-sized sections for you to absorb at your own pace. Feel free to take notes or highlight any passages which speak to your heart to reflect on later.

Why We Suffer as Empaths

Have you ever wondered why you struggle to maintain healthy boundaries, stay grounded, or differentiate your emotions from other's emotions as an empath? Have you ever tried to figure out why you give so much of yourself to other people to the point of burnout and sometimes even emotional meltdown?

Psychiatrist and psychoanalyst Carl Jung developed a theory in the early 20th century that explains why we struggle so much as empaths. This theory was called the process of individuation.

Individuation, as Jung put it in one of his lectures, is "the psychological process that makes of a human being an individual – a unique, indivisible unit or 'whole man'." In other words, individuation is the process of cultivating wholeness and becoming our authentic and true selves.

Not only is individuation the process of becoming a fully mature human being, but it is also the process of finding our essence, our very Souls. However, when this process of individuation gets disrupted within us due to various life experiences, we end up developing a weak sense of self and a tenuous grip on reality.

Every empath that struggles with absorbing other people's emotions has struggled to complete their individuation process. When this process of psychological and emotional growth is disturbed, we begin confusing other's emotions as our own, setting poor boundaries, sacrificing our needs, attracting narcissists and energy vampires, and falling into toxic behavioral patterns. Therefore, your mission as an empath is to become a fully individuated person by incorporating the practices mentioned in this chapter into your life.

Practice 1 – Self-Responsibility

Self-responsibility is the very first practice of individuation. Without taking responsibility for our growth, wellbeing, happiness, and fulfillment, we end up stranded in a stagnating pool of unhappiness. It's very easy to blame other people for our pain, but at the end of the day, we are the rulers of our lives. The power is in our hands to decide to take responsibility for our wellbeing, or avoid that responsibility through blame, evasion, projection, and addiction. But taking responsibility for our empowerment can be scary and sometimes difficult, there's no doubt about it. After all, we're essentially holding ourselves accountable for all the decisions and mindsets we decide to adopt. It's much less daunting to hold *other* people accountable for our unhappiness because we don't cop the blame, and therefore, we don't have to deal with the shame!

But while taking responsibility for your wellbeing can be hard, it is also extremely empowering and invigorating. When you carry self-responsibility you are giving yourself the ability to grow, heal, and mature as an empath. You're basically giving yourself the key to achieving your true and highest potential! But the truth is that, deep down, many of us fear stepping into our power and highest potential. We are so overcome with toxic core beliefs that we feel that we don't deserve to be strong, wise, compassionate, and enlightened human beings.

Spiritual teacher Marianne Williamson has a beautiful quote that elucidates this reality:

"Our deepest fear is not that we are inadequate. Our deepest fear is that we are powerful beyond measure. It is our light not our darkness that most frightens us. We ask ourselves, who am I to be brilliant, gorgeous, talented and fabulous? Actually, who are you not to be? You are a child of God. Your playing small does not serve the world. There's nothing enlightened about shrinking so that other people won't feel insecure around you. We were born to make manifest the glory of God that is within us."[1]

As an empath, you were born with a rare and precious gift. It's time for you to step up and reclaim your power.

Practice 2 – Sending Back Energy

"I'm an empath. What I normally do is take some of my partner's emotional pain away by letting her release it onto me. Right now she doesn't want to be healed, she's kept in her emotions too long and I can feel it, but I want this pain to go away so we can go back to our normal selves. So how do I properly heal her?" **– Liam, empath reader from lonerwolf.com**

Self-responsibility is a two way street. Not only does being accountable for your health and happiness mean being responsible for yourself, but it also means allowing other people to take responsibility for themselves.

We have a tendency as empaths to carry the weight of the world on our shoulders. Because of our deeply empathic natures, we feel cruel when we don't help others in great pain, and so we tend to automatically take on their burdens. But there is a big difference between helping others and literally taking on their emotional pain. We need to understand that it is

208

NOT our job to take on the pain of others. So many empaths out there have shared with me the mistaken belief that they believe they were *made* to be martyrs, as if it's their life purpose to take away the pain of people and bear it themselves. But there is no glory in being a martyr, especially if you are taking away the very thing that other people need to grow: their pain.

It is in no way, shape or form your cosmic duty or responsibility to take away the pain of other people. This is because by absorbing the pain of others, you are depriving them of a vital element of their spiritual evolution and karmic responsibility. For example, when you take on the frustration of another person, you are essentially removing the key they need to make significant life changes. How can that person decide that they need to find a more fulfilling life path without their frustration to wake them up? If we take on the sadness of another person, how can that person fully learn how to love and take care of themselves? If we take on the anger of another person, how can that person learn the lesson of self-regulating their emotions and improving their relationships? Without these emotions, these people would likely continue their unhealthy patterns of behavior, resulting in all types of prolonged personal and interpersonal issues.

The truth is that we are not here to be sponges or enablers. We are here to be helpers, guides, and supporters.

It's true that we aren't always conscious of our tendency to absorb other's pain, but once we *are* aware of this tendency it is up to us to no longer take on the emotions of others. The very best thing we can do for others isn't soaking up their pain; it is actually holding space for them. Holding space for a person means giving them the room to grieve or vent while still maintaining our own boundaries. Holding space for others is about supporting others through non-judgmental presence, acknowledging that you are simply playing the role of a compassionate confidant – not a self-sacrificing martyr.

When we understand that emotions of other people serve as messengers, challenges, and opportunities to look within, we're able to release ourselves of the burden of consciously or unconsciously absorbing their emotions. The fact is that, no matter how painful, people *need* their emotions as an impetus to grow mentally, emotionally, and spiritually. It is not your place to take that from them.

But what do we do when we've already absorbed the emotional and physical energy of others? How can we release the murky and oppressive feelings within us?

One of the best methods out there is what I call the Sending Back Energy Visualization (SBEV). Here is how to practice this powerful visualization:

Step 1 – Sit or lie down in a quiet place, and begin to relax.
Step 2 – Gently focus on deepening your in-breath and out-breath to whatever rhythm feels the most natural to you.
Step 3 – Once you are breathing deeply, start focusing on the sensations in your body. In what places does your body feel tense, heavy, aching, sore or numb? Do your head, shoulders, eyebrows, chest, stomach, back, hands or legs feel sore? Notice the feelings in your body and see that they are places where emotions have been stored.
Step 4 – Once you are aware of sore or heavy areas within your body, begin to visualize the emotions being stored in those places coming out of your body in streams or ribbons of color. For example, you might visualize the tension in your

neck as a stream of red or orange. Or you might visualize the suffocating feeling in your chest as a stream of black coming out of your body. Feel free to use dark and murky colors for negative emotions.

Step 5 – As the stream of color floats above your body repeat to yourself, "I send this energy back to whomever it belongs to with love and kindness." Then, visualize the stream of color flying off into the distance and dissolving.

Step 6 – Once you have sent back the energy, scan your body for any other painful feelings that you can visualize and release. Please note that it's also possible to absorb the positive energy of others, so you're welcome to see what positive energy feels foreign to you, and release that as well.

Step 7 – Once your body feels energetically "empty," it is now time to send your body loving and healing energy. You can repeat the mantra, "I love you" to every part in your body that was carrying the burden of other's energy with sincerity. Alternatively, you can visualize a warm violet ball of light filling your whole body with peace and wellbeing.

Step 8 – Once you are finished, allow yourself to be still for a few minutes to integrate your new emotional cleansing.

This visualization can be repeated as many times as you like throughout the day. It's also important to remember that while doing the Sending Back Energy Visualization you allow the energy to return to whomever it came from, without naming anyone in particular. Sometimes we are not completely conscious of *who* exactly our energetic debris came from, therefore, we don't want to make the mistake of sending this energy to the wrong person! Even if we're ninety nine percent sure that our emotions came from a certain person, it's better to let the energy, by itself, instinctively return to whomever it came from. Trust in the Universe's intelligence.

Practice 3 – Setting Boundaries

Ultimately, there are two main approaches to healing as an empath: the first approach is to surrender, and the second approach is to assertively create boundaries. In this section we'll explore the necessity to create boundaries, and in the next chapter we'll explore surrender.

The path of healing requires balance: we need to create boundaries so we don't become emotional sponges, but we also need to surrender so that we don't become too constrained in our self-made boundaries.

Unfortunately, in the empath community, creating boundaries is often approached with a fearful mindset instead of the desire to become fully mature and individuated beings. This fearful mindset often gives rise to terms such as "protection," "cloaking," "shielding," and so forth. Instead of using empowering terms, we empaths tend to use phrases that suggest minimizing or hiding ourselves away from others instead of stepping into our natural power.

Don't get me wrong, while "shielding" and "cloaking" techniques can be useful practices, they are very temporary in nature. I only ever recommend shielding and cloaking as temporary practices for untrained empaths who are extremely overwhelmed by the world, and this is because shielding/cloaking are both too difficult to sustain for long periods of time. Our natural tendency is to flow with life, not to constantly resist it and put up a wall against it.

The much better long term solution I recommend for empaths who struggle with issues such as anxiety, emotional contagion, codependence, and constant absorption energy is the creation of boundaries. Setting boundaries is more of a mindset than it is a technique. In other words, setting boundaries requires you to change the way you perceive and value your energetic space.

Setting boundaries is an absolutely mandatory practice as an empath. Likely, one of the main reasons why you're reading this book in the first place is because you're struggling with some kind of energetic boundary issue. When you learn how to establish, and respect, your own boundaries, you complete the process of individuation – developing a strong and balanced sense of self.

In fact, almost every problem we have as empaths can be traced back to our weak or absent energetic boundaries. Just as the body needs the skin as a physical boundary that keeps us in good health, so too do we need an "energy skin" that preserves and supports our emotional and mental health.

The main reason why we need energetic boundaries or an energy skin is so that we're able to distinguish between our own emotions and thoughts, and those of others. This ability to discover what energy is ours helps us to remain grounded, centered, and emotionally balanced. And when we're emotionally balanced, we can see life with clarity, making it easier for us to align with our Souls.

Like physical human skin, energy boundaries help us to maintain an important barrier between foreign allergens and bacteria in the form of other people's emotional and mental energy. When we lack this skin, we're constantly exposing ourselves to emotional pathogens which we absorb and carry around with us, sometimes for years.

Creating energetic boundaries can take time and practice. Often, we need to be exposed to many different types of situations before we have strong and "weathered" energy skin. So don't be disheartened if you struggle at first. However, if you persist in trying to create a strong energy skin, your discipline will be greatly rewarded and you'll find yourself gaining more energy, confidence, and inner fulfillment than ever before.

Here are some tips and practices you can incorporate into your life which will help you create and maintain energetic boundaries:

1. Stop trying to fix people.

As empaths, we have the tendency to want to fix and help everyone at all times. While it's good that we help others, we need to remember that our wellbeing is important as well. Not only that, but it isn't actually our place to "fix" other people. While we can offer our guidance and a shoulder to cry on, our responsibility does not lie in fixing others and their problems. We need to draw the line when it comes to giving help and remember that other people must ultimately take responsibility for their happiness, not us.

2. Identify physical, emotional, and psychological violations.

Make a list of situations throughout your day that make you feel physically, emotionally or psychologically uncomfortable or "used." For example, did someone touch you without your permission, take your belongings, or simply come too close to you, making you feel exposed? Did someone make fun of you, ask you for too many favors, or manipulate you in any way that made you feel vulnerable? Write a list every day of people and situations which you feel have violated your energetic boundaries. The more aware you become of these situations, the better equipped you'll be to draw the line.

3. Learn how to say "no."

There's no doubt about it, saying "no" to people can be scary and strange territory. As empaths, we're so used to saying "yes" without thinking that we tend to associate the denial of other people's requests as a bad or selfish act. Usually, our inability to say no goes all the way back to childhood when we were taught the mistaken belief that we should always extend our help to others, no matter what. If we didn't, we were taught that this behavior was "self-centered" and therefore condemnable.

As adults, we need to be aware of this mistaken belief undermining a lot of our thinking patterns. While saying no all the time to other people is unhealthy, there are many situations in life where we actually need to say "no" for our own wellbeing, or for the health of our other relationships.

For example, is it healthy to always say "yes" to your boss when you know it will negatively impact your connection with your family? Of course not. There are some situations in life that require a firm "no."

Learning how to say no is essentially a form of self-love because it acknowledges that your needs are just as valuable and relevant as other people's needs. If you struggle to say a flat out "no," you can adjust this phrase into a sentence such as "I'm sorry, I can't," "I'm not able to do that, maybe

215

tomorrow," "I'm feeling tired today, maybe another week," "Not today," and so forth.

4. Breathe properly.

Strangely enough, one of the quickest ways to become ungrounded and lose touch with your boundaries is through not breathing properly. In the West, we have the habit of breathing from our chests instead of our bellies. When we breathe shallowly through our chests, we limit the flow of oxygen through our body, making it easier for us to become anxious and lightheaded.

The proper and natural way to breathe is actually deeply, through your stomach in what is called a "belly breath." When you breathe deeply, you stimulate the vagus nerve in your body, which alerts receptors in your brain to calm down your body's nervous system. When your nervous system is relaxed, you will find it much easier to maintain your energetic boundaries.

If you're new to deep breathing, you can try the easy four seconds in, and four seconds out breathing technique. Simply breathe slowly for four seconds, and then breathe out slowly for four seconds. Make sure your stomach expands when you breathe. You can use this technique wherever you are and in any situation throughout the day.

Eventually, you can even try more advanced breathing techniques such as those used in Pranayama which are styles of breathing used in yoga. These breathing techniques can calm your nervous and endocrine system, create more mental alertness, and even infuse your body with more energy.

5. Give yourself permission to practice self-care.

Creating and maintaining healthy energetic boundaries is about treating yourself with love and respect. Without self-respect, you'll constantly allow others and their energy to overstep your boundaries and interfere with your life.

One of the biggest struggles that arise among our students are the feelings of guilt that are triggered from self-care. As one woman related to me, "Every time I try to step away from others and what they ask from me I'm instantly hit with this gargantuan wave of guilt that almost leaves me numb." The best way to overcome this guilt is by creating affirmations or practicing the socratic questioning technique mentioned in the last chapter. For example, whenever this guilt arises you can practice repeating the mantra, "It's OK to take care of my needs, I am worthy," or whatever mantra you find fitting.

Self-care comes in many shapes and forms. It can be as simple as treating yourself to a nice massage or taking a break from work, to as complex as setting specific time restraints with people who leech your energy. In whatever circumstance, self-care is always about learning to step away and cater to whatever needs you have in the moment.

6. Notice and prepare for triggers.

There are many situations in our lives which trigger the weakening of our boundaries. As empaths, some of the most common boundary-weakening situations involve extreme emotions such as grief and anger from others, romantic relationships, family obligations, and crowded or congested places full of people. It's important that you identify your own personal triggers by paying close attention to your emotions

217

and the physical sensations inside your body. You might like to ask yourself, "What is this person doing/what am I doing that is triggering these feelings?" "What has changed in my surroundings that might be triggering these emotions?"

Make a mental note of your triggers and be conscious of them so that you can be more mindful in the future. You might like to journal about your triggers to understand them better.

7. Say a power prayer.

It is my belief that the Universe is always receptive to our needs. In other words, when we pray, we're essentially sending a very clear message to the Universe that we need guidance and support.

A prayer itself is condensed energy that comes from the heart. What better way to communicate your deepest needs and desires? What could be more powerful than a prayer? Yet prayer is something we so often overlook or use as a "last resort" when we've exhausted all other options.

Since incorporating the power of prayer into my life on a regular basis, I've experienced titanic shifts and spurts of growth that have permanently changed my life for the better. As an empath, I regularly pray about creating inner harmony and learning how to access my inner power.

Here is a sample prayer you can use in your own life about creating boundaries:

Dear Life/God/Goddess/Universe/Soul, please help me to create and maintain healthy boundaries that will enable be to live a more balanced life. Help me to respect my needs and be assertive in overwhelming situations. Guide me in creating a strong and clear sense of self. Amen.

The more frequently you pray from the heart, the more miracles you will witness in your life.

Practice 4 – Emotional Discernment

In order to heal ourselves on an emotional level as empaths, we need to learn the vital life skill of emotional discernment. In many ways, emotional discernment comes as a natural product of creating healthy and well-defined energetic boundaries. However, there are a few practices we can learn that will help support our process of creating a healthy sense of self.

Most empaths, in some form, struggle with emotional discernment. Our inability to identify what is "our stuff" versus what is "other's stuff" lies at the heart of our energetic confusion, and the more we're confused, the more unnecessary baggage we take on.

How often have felt completely fine one minute, and like a train wreck the next? How often have you sat down at the end of the day and felt energetically dirty, as though a cloud of smog has possessed your body? How many times have you only just managed to drag yourself through an exhausting day and felt completely frail?

If you're struggling with murky, muddy, and draining emotions on a daily basis, you likely lack emotional discernment. While all of the advice we've given in this book so far will help you to learn the skill of emotional discernment, there are a few other practices which we recommend specifically for this issue:

219

- Learn how to anchor and ground yourself into the present moment through your breath. Practice slow and deep breathing.
- Practice self-awareness throughout your day: pay attention to how you feel and what you're thinking.
- Ask yourself, "Why am I feeling this way?" "When did these sensations arise?" "Did this feeling come from one of my thoughts, or did it come from someone I interacted with?" "How does this place make me feel?" "What do I intuitively feel about this person or place?"
- Make a habit of journaling about your emotions versus other people's emotions. For example, you might like to write down a few emotions you experienced during the day, and next to each one whether the feeling originated from you or someone else. For instance, "Anger from 9:30am to 11am = Came from my work colleagues. Overwhelming anxiety at 4pm = Came from me because of my deadline. Jealousy 7pm = Came from a friend I spoke with on the phone."
- Be careful of projection; the tendency to unconsciously disown and attribute your emotions to other people. Make sure that an emotion is truly originating from another by asking yourself, "Are any of my inner fears contributing to my feelings?" Be honest.
- Usually the emotional energy within you will be a mixture of your own and other people's energy. To find more clarity, try giving a percentage to what you feel. For example, 65% of what I feel is mine and 35% is from other people.

Once you have managed to discern how much of the energy within you is foreign, you can then practice a technique such as the Sending Back Energy Visualization (SBEV). If you're short on time, you can simply ground and revitalize your body through your breath.

We'll explore even more powerful techniques in the next chapter.

Practice 5 – Cutting Ties With Toxic People

It is our nature as empaths to be emotionally attentive, receptive, and empathetic towards others. Unfortunately, this very sensitivity can lead us to making too many energetic commitments to people who demand more from us than we can give. Sometimes these people are well-meaning but needy friends, associates, and family members. Other times, these people are deeply wounded "energy vampires" who desperately need help. And sometimes, these demanding people are predatory narcissists who are attracted to our vulnerabilities like an animal is to fresh meat.

With all of these draining connections and nagging responsibilities, it's no wonder that we suffer from chronic mental and physical illnesses such as chronic fatigue syndrome, fibromyalgia, and anxiety disorders.

A major part of taking responsibility for your happiness and creating strong energetic boundaries is learning how to take inventory of your connections and determine which people need to be removed ASAP. While cutting people away from your life may feel harsh or extreme, it doesn't need to be a dramatic process. In fact, it's very possible to remove people with your life with absolute compassion and love for them while remembering that they are not compatible with your current life path.

Without a doubt, removing people from your life can be a difficult and emotional process, particularly if you're in a codependent relationship and your happiness relies on their wellbeing. However, without actively "weeding" your social and emotional garden, you will continue to feel drained, taken advantage of, and used. You will never be able to reach your true potential with dead weight hanging from you.

In my own experience, as well as that of many of the empaths I have mentored, cutting ties with toxic people is a truly liberating step which is vital for our wellbeing. Usually, when we're feeling exhausted, depressed, and overwhelmed, we don't actually have the capacity to genuinely help others in the first place. So while we may crave to help the needy, wounded people in our lives, we first must be able to heal ourselves. As the biblical proverb goes, "Healer, heal thyself." Therefore, first, we must be able to heal ourselves before we can truly heal others. And usually, this healing process requires space and a certain level of solitude.

As Joseph, an empath and clinical psychologist shared with me, "I was so wound up in the lives and problems of my clients that I was ignoring all the red flags that my own mental health was on the decline. These people I cared about on a daily basis consumed so much of my time that I had nothing left to give to myself. I was completely wiped out to the point of an almost emotional breakdown, and I didn't even realize it."

The sad thing that many of us empaths don't realize is that often our desire to heal others is a disguised cry for help for our own healing. Because many of us weren't taught how to value or nurture ourselves at a young age, we tend to unconsciously seek out our own healing in the healing of others. Obviously, this approach to healing eventually leads us

222

into codependent relationships and enabling roles in life that we struggle to extract ourselves from.

So the question is, have you projected your need to heal into the people around you? Is it possible that your desire to help others is actually a form of self-avoidance to mask the emptiness you feel inside? Are you giving other people what you have always desired for yourself? I recommend that you seriously sit down and journal about these questions, because the answer might surprise you and potentially change your life.

Here are some other practices you can use to help you free up more emotional space by removing energy-draining people from your life:

1. Make a list.

Make a list of all the people you regularly interact with every week. These people could be your family or extended family, spouse, children, friends, acquaintances or work colleagues. Separate the people on your list into three sections: people to keep in your life, people to remove from your life, and people you're unsure about.

2. Ask, "What is this person contributing to my life?"

With the people you're unsure about, ask what they are contributing to your life. In other words, are they only *taking* from you, or are they giving you something valuable in return? For example, they might positively contribute to your life a sense of humor, a compassionate heart, their time, their advice or anything else which lifts your spirits. On the other hand, they might negatively contribute to your life by causing you self-doubt, taking up your time, asking too many favors, exhausting your energy or triggering dark emotions in you.

On a piece of paper, draw a line down the middle and separate the page into two sides. On the left side, list all of the positive things the person you're unsure about brings to your life. On the right side, list all of the negative contributions they bring. Once you're done, weigh up both sides: which side outweighs the other? If you have a balance of positive and negative qualities, ask yourself, do you have the time and energy to include this person in your life right now? Would you be better off keeping them around or letting them go?

Remember, healthy relationships involve a balanced percentage of give and take. In order to live an intentional and empowered life as an empath, you need to be able to justify why the people in your life are there, and what exactly they bring to the table.

3. Identify toxic behavior.

There are about eight different types of toxic behavior in people that can limit your growth as an empath. Keep an eye out for the following kind of people in your life:

- The Grudge-Holder – these are people who refuse to forgive you and constantly carry bitter grudges and resentments
- The Complainer – these people are forever complaining about everything and anything all day long
- The Critic – these people are extremely judgmental and you will find it hard to be yourself around them because they are forever criticizing you or other people

- The Downer – these people are forever seeing the negative side of life and are oppressive and depressing to be around
- The Manipulator – these people use you in order to gain something and they often use tactics such as exploitation, blackmail, and deceit to get what they want from you
- The Taker – these people take your time, attention, energy, and sometimes even money without giving anything to you in return
- The Unsupporter – these people are not truly interested in supporting your goals or dreams and pressure you to be like everyone else
- The Drama Queen/King – these people are addicted to creating and sustaining drama as a way of filling a source of emptiness inside

Once you're able to identify these limiting and destructive behavioral patterns in people, you can then determine who to keep and who to cut off from your life.

4. Use one of these three approaches.

Once you have decided that a person or group of people need to be removed from your life, you can use one of three approaches. The first approach is to slowly cut off contact. For example, you can gradually deny their requests to go out, stop answering their messages and calls so often, and make other plans that will prevent you from seeing them.

The second approach is to speak with the person you intend to cut off contact with. You can explain to them why you need space and think that parting ways will be the best. I only recommend this approach with very close friends or family members because you must have a strong emotional connection to begin with to make this approach worth it. For example, this approach can be used with one of your parents, romantic partners or siblings as a form of respect for them. Sometimes expressing your thoughts to those close to you is better than complete silence which creates a lot of confusion and suffering in others. However, you do need to be emotionally and energetically prepared for backlash from them about your choice. If face-to-face contact is too difficult, you can consider writing a letter to them instead.

The third approach is the swift and quick removal of people from your life. I recommend this approach for particularly toxic relationships such as those we sometimes have with narcissists, energy vampires or abusive people. With this approach, you need to "rip the bandaid off" as quickly as you can and sever all contact with them. You may, for instance, choose to block their social media account and phone number, change address, ignore their attempts to contact you, or even change jobs if the situation is extreme enough.

Finally, be kind with yourself and if necessary, give yourself the space to grieve the person's loss. As an empath, it is normal to experience some level of guilt and even selfishness for ending toxic relationships. But remember, cutting off certain people is about self-respect and honoring your need to grow into the person you're destined to become.

Practice 6 – Etheric Cord Cutting

Another emotionally healing practice that you can apply to ending connections with people is called Etheric Cord Cutting. Etheric cords are the energy structures in our bodies that link us to other people. An Etheric cord itself looks like a tube or hose of energy that extends out of the body and links us with other people. Because an etheric cord is not limited by space or distance, we can be connected to people who are miles away and even on different continents.

We all possess etheric cords, but the strongest cords we possess are with those whom we have had, or continue to have, emotional or sexual connections with. Usually, our etheric cords are the strongest with our friends, siblings, parents, ex-spouses, children, work colleagues, and current romantic partners.

Etheric cords themselves can be healthy or unhealthy. Energy moves along these tubes and is exchanged between us and other people, meaning that we can access the energy fields of others, and vice versa. In this sense, etheric cords are like energetic regulation and feedback systems. When these etheric cords become unhealthy due to fear, anger, resentments, jealousy, low self-esteem, and codependency issues, our energy easily becomes drained and imbalanced. Any relationship in which a person looks to another for their source of light and happiness is a relationship that tends to develop unhealthy etheric cords.

At any one time we can have dozens of negative etheric cords attached to us. One of the easiest ways to determine whether you have a dysfunctional etheric cord is how often you think about a person, and what emotions they provoke in you. Are there any people in your life whom you constantly think about with sadness, anger, resentment, longing or fear? If so, you've likely got thick etheric cords connected to them.

Not only that, but if you're in a healing profession, you've also likely got negative etheric cords attached to you. Many caregivers, therapists, social workers, spiritual mentors, and other people in caring professions have cords attached to them from needy people who they help on a daily basis. Through these cords, energy can be pumped into you or sucked out of you without your conscious awareness or even proximity to these people. In the English language, we tend to describe these etheric connections as negative "emotional attachments."

So what is the answer? How can we stop our energy being siphoned through these etheric cords without our conscious awareness?

One of the best practices out there that can supplement the other practices mentioned in this chapter is called Etheric Cord Cutting. Cord cutting allows you to release the negative emotional attachments you have to others while still loving and caring for them in a healthy way.

Here, it's important to note that Etheric Cord Cutting **does not** mean that your relationships will break apart or you will stop caring for those closest to you in any way. Instead, cord cutting is about removing sick and dysfunctional energetic cords that perpetuate feelings of codependency, fear, and exhaustion between you and other people.

Here is how to practice Etheric Cord Cutting:

1. Sit or stand in a quiet place.
2. Breathe deeply and slowly into your stomach to relax your body.

3. Once you're relaxed, imagine the areas of your body where negative cords might be attached. Focus on places in your body that feel sore, heavy or numb. It doesn't matter if you don't know where your cords are attached, this practice will still be effective.

4. Once you have located your cords, visualize a large golden sword in your hand. This sword will be used to cut your etheric cords.

5. Say a prayer and ask your Soul or spirit guides to help you remove all etheric cords that do not serve your highest good. For example, "Dear Soul, please help me remove any toxic etheric cords that are draining my energy. Amen." Alternatively, you can say to yourself a mantra while you cut the cords such as "I now release all fear-based attachments."

6. Bring your hand with the sword over the areas of your body that have etheric cords. You can even imagine the sound of cutting if it helps.

7. Once you have finished cutting, imagine a white light of purification soaking into your head and throughout your entire body, and expanding outwards into your aura or energy field. Continue to breathe deeply and allow yourself to integrate the experience.

Even if you struggle to visualize your cords or cutting them away, be assured that this simple exercise will still work if you are sincere about it.

Practice 7 – Self-Love

"I have a hard time staying away from those that need love when I desperately need to take the time to love myself more."
– Harmony, empath reader from lonerwolf.com

Having the highest possible vibration of any emotion or experience, love is the secret key to growth and rapid transformation. Without love, all of our efforts to find peace, balance, and empowerment fail, over and over again. While it's important that we learn and master different techniques, the moment we infuse all that we do with self-love is the moment we truly start experiencing authentic change.

True healing and empowerment is about opening your heart to love. This love that I speak of isn't the warm, fuzzy, or sentimental notion of love that most people believe in and propagate. Instead, this love is fierce, strong, and unconditionally accepting. Unconditional acceptance means that no matter what you feel, think, say or do, you are still accepted and cherished by your heart, just as you are.

Genuine self-love is the most profound experience in the universe. However, it usually takes time, sincere dedication, and discipline to develop. We are surrounded by so many images, beliefs, and behaviors that reinforce the idea of self-hatred every day that it can be extremely difficult for us to connect to the love inside of us. How often have you watched movies or read magazines, books, or newspapers that supported the idea of the "perfect life"? How often have you gone on social media and felt depressed by other people and their seemingly "ideal" lives (or at least, what they choose to share)?

Left, right, and center, we are constantly made to feel that we aren't good enough. Social institutions and structures, knowing about this innate human vulnerability, use this self-doubt as a "tool" to coerce us. So it's no surprise that the majority of human beings on this planet suffer from the underlying core belief that "I'm not good enough." Everywhere we go, this idea is eternally reinforced!

As an empath, you feel this self-loathing perhaps more intensely than anyone else. Not only can you sense the negative vibrational energy of others, but you also feel "not good enough" in your ability to deal with life. Society and childhood traumas have left you feeling like there is something profoundly, innately messed up or emotionally "handicapped" about you. And the more people you come in contact with, the more this ingrained belief is strengthened. The way you have been made to feel about yourself is further bolstered by negative self-talk, which create negative beliefs, and eventually, a negative mental lens through which you perceive yourself.

In this book so far we have explored how to explore these mistaken and core beliefs you may have about yourself. We've also explored many different forms of self-love such as taking care of your body, setting boundaries, creating affirmations, sending back energy, and much more. However, we haven't yet explored the fundamental core of self-love itself: unconditional acceptance.

What is Unconditional Acceptance?

Unconditional acceptance literally means accepting yourself without conditions. In normal day to day life, we tend to "love" ourselves in a very conditional way. For example, we'll only celebrate ourselves when we've experienced some form of success or embrace our emotions when we're feeling happy and upbeat. We'll even base our value on how much other people approve of us through their compliments or rewards, and only *then* accept our amazing gifts. But what happens

231

when we feel depressed, angry, shamed, inferior or used in some way? In the moments when we need love the most, we abandon ourselves. Not only do we abandon ourselves, but we even attack ourselves with hateful thoughts and unkind words. How often has someone hurt you, and instead of comforting yourself, you thought "Yeah, I deserve that," or "I'm such an idiot, what was I thinking?"

In many situations, we become our own worst enemies. Not only do we feel overwhelmed and inundated by other's energy, but we also feel trapped in our minds – and there is no comfort or solace within our minds. There is only fear, insecurity, and judgment. This sad state of affairs leads to an imprisoned and hellish life where our only escape is through some kind of addiction, form of escapism or numbing habit.

One of the saddest things I ever heard was from a mother who was learning how to identify her core beliefs. She told me, "All I feel is fear, and I don't know where to run anymore. There are enemies without me and enemies within me. There is no solace anywhere."

As we can see, the mind is like an endless abyss. The pursuit of seeking approval from other people only deepens this abyss because the search is never-ending. The moment we think we've gained love or acceptance from another person is the moment we have to put all of our effort into maintaining that love. But the truth that many of us empaths forget is that any source of love or acceptance outside of ourselves can be taken away as quickly as it was obtained. One moment someone may like you, and the next, they might hate you. One moment you may have a friend, and the next, you may have an enemy.

It's not within our power to maintain the approval of others. We cannot force others to like us. We cannot always predict what will make a person dislike us. But it *is* within our power to approve of ourselves, no matter what. This is called unconditional acceptance.

Unconditional acceptance is at the core of self-love. It means that no matter what you think, say, do or feel, you will still support, care for, and nurture yourself. "How is this possible?" you may think. The answer is that the only way to unconditionally accept ourselves is through the door of the Heart, not the mind.

How to Develop Self-Love

Almost all empaths that I have come across or mentored have struggled with heart chakra problems. The heart chakra, or energy center located within your heart region, is responsible for giving and receiving love. Most empaths have no problem giving love … to *other* people. But when it comes to giving love to and receiving love from themselves, there is a great struggle.

There are two kinds of heart chakra issues: the first is an underactive heart chakra, and the second is an overactive heart chakra. Both underactive and overactive chakra issues are to do with the energy regulation, and how much energy is permitted to enter the heart chakra region. When too much energy enters the heart chakra, the result is an overactive heart. An overactive heart manifests as:

- codependency
- poor boundaries
- manipulative tendencies

- emotional explosiveness
- susceptibility to being ruled by emotions

An underactive heart, on the other hand, manifests as:

- the tendency to withdraw from others
- emotional coldness
- a feeling of alienation
- persistent loneliness
- difficulty in opening up to others

Most empaths that I've met have an overactive heart chakra, though not all of them. Take a moment to consider your own heart. Which list of signs can you identify the most with? Do you have an underactive or an overactive heart chakra? Of course, most of us share both overactive and underactive symptoms, but there is usually a predominance in one over the other.

Although they appear to be very different, underactive and overactive heart chakras both need the same antidote: the development of unconditional self-love. Self-love helps the heart to both open as well as helping it to respect its own needs and boundaries.

By accessing and learning to live from the heart in a balanced way, we bless all that we do. The more we learn to live from a place of deep self-love, the more we will feel safe, open, and respected, no matter where we are, what is happening to us or how other people are treating us.

Can you imagine what life would feel like if you always held within your heart a place of warmth and solace? Can you imagine what it would be like to live in the world with your heart open and unafraid, because everything you need is within you? What I am describing here is not an ideal: it is a reality that we have all lost touch with. In order to drink from the wellsprings of our hearts, we need to cut through the illusions in our lives.

Within us all there is a place that transcends the mind, the body, and the personality. This place exists behind your thoughts and emotions, and is the wise observer of all that you do. Through the ages, prophets, sages, mystics, shamans, and wise elders have called this place God, Goddess, Shiva, the Higher Self, Consciousness, I AM, Spirit, Soul, and thousands of other names. Practicing unconditional self-love and acceptance is about accessing this eternal part of who you are. Through the door of the Heart, you will be able to contact your deepest Nature and live from a place of emotional balance – no matter *what* arises.

Here are some of the most powerful practices for developing unconditional self-love (other than what has already been recommended in this book):

1. Practice Soul Gazing.

Surprisingly, this exercise can be very confronting for a lot of people. But let's face it: this exercise can feel a bit odd at first! Looking deeply into your own eyes is one of the most candid and honest ways you can access your self-love. If you find that looking into your own eyes is difficult, this is most likely a sign that you are struggling to tune into your deeper self. Feelings of shame, sadness, anger or embarrassment signify that you are harboring repressed inner emotions towards yourself. These emotions are often rooted in low self-worth or self-hatred.

To overcome these difficult feelings, try practicing this exercise every day for five minutes. You're welcome to increase the amount of time you spend doing this practice through time to ten, even twenty minutes or more. Begin the practice by situating yourself in front of a mirror. You may like to sit or stand, depending on which position is more comfortable for you. As you relax, gaze into your eyes gently. It is normal if you feel uncomfortable sensations emerge within you, but go with them: accept them as they are. As you gaze softly into your eyes, try to feel the eternal presence within you, gazing back at you. Feel the wisdom in your eyes, the love, and understanding slowly emerging through your irises.

Sometimes it can take a few practices to connect with your deeper self. For example, you might struggle with a lot of sadness or grief as you gaze into your eyes. Instead of pushing away this sadness, hold it in gentle awareness. You may even like to comfort yourself verbally or mentally by saying, "It's OK. I love and support you." In fact, your Soul Gazing practice will deepen when you can look deeply into your own eyes and say kind words. You may even like to hug yourself as you practice Soul Gazing. Do whatever feels the most organic to you.

It is common to discover many hidden or repressed thoughts and emotions through this practice, so make sure you write down whatever you discover afterwards to explore further.

2. Contact your Divine Inner Mother or Father.

There are many faces of our Souls. One of these faces is what I call the Divine Mother or Father. The Divine Mother or Father is similar to a human parent, but the difference is that the

Divine Mother/Father is unconditionally loving and present with you in each and every moment. In other words, no matter where you are, what you are doing or how you are feeling, the Divine Mother/Father is always present, even if you can't perceive them. In essence, the Divine Mother or Father is the embodiment of unconditional acceptance and love. No matter what you think, say, feel or do, your Divine inner Mother or Father still loves you without conditions.

If you experienced a traumatic childhood, suffered from a broken household or the absence of a mother or father, discovering the presence of the Divine Mother or Father can be life-changing. The moment I came in contact with my inner Divine Mother was the moment true self-love grew. I had been staring into the mirror for half an hour crying after experiencing intense and crippling anxiety when suddenly, a warm presence emerged within my eyes. Suddenly I knew I was loved no matter what I felt, thought or did by this mysterious presence within me. The only human experience I could compare this love to was the love felt by a Mother or Father towards their child … but even that experience seemed lacking. This love was beyond anything I had ever experienced. It was one of the most profound experiences of my life.

Since then, I've learned that the Inner Mother or Father can be contacted in any moment. Not only that, but the more you engage with your Inner Mother or Father, the more he/she spontaneously arises when you need him/her the moment.

Here are some ways to contact and engage with your Divine inner Parent:

- Practice Soul Gazing
- Connect with your breath

- Say a prayer asking for guidance from your inner Mother/Father
- Sit quietly alone and feel the presence of your Divine Mother/Father
- Visualize meeting your divine Mother/Father
- Draw your Divine Mother/Father
- Channel your Divine Mother/Father through writing

It also helps if you decide what gender your divine inner parent will be: male or female. For example, as a female, I feel more naturally drawn to the Divine Mother. However, you might be different depending on what gender you are and your early life experiences.

Remember, the Divine Mother/Father is not separate from you: it is one face of your True Nature.

3. Allow yourself to feel *everything* without identification.

Unconditional self-love is about honoring and making space for *all* human experience, including every type of emotion and thought. As an empath, it's vital that you learn how to hold space for your emotions, even the most painful ones. By anchoring yourself in your breath, you can learn how to witness the emotional energy of others within you, without attaching yourself to these sensations. Remember, the emotions you experience are passing and in no way reflect the truth of you who are. How can they when they are so changeable and transient?

Value all emotions just as they are. The more you hide from, deny, or hate what you feel, the more you will suffer. In fact, the very act of repressing or trying to change what you're feeling is an act of emotional violence. Allow everything, and

238

repress nothing. Let the love within you cradle you through emotions such as anger, resentment, jealousy, anxiety, or whatever other people transmit. Even when you get sucked up into the whirlpool of identification, connect with your breath again to ground yourself.

4. Practice loving all that arises.

Every thought, feeling, and sensation within your body throughout the day offers you an opportunity to love. Good or bad, whatever you experience is a lesson or a reminder to connect with love. Remember, unconditional love isn't the mushy or sentimental romantic love we so often picture. Instead, unconditional love is absolute openness and acceptance of everything. Even the *inability* to be loving can be loved!

Practicing loving all that arises is an unending journey that will deepen your relationship with unconditional love more and more. While this practice is perhaps the most difficult in existence, it is also the most worthy of your time and effort. I can't express how profoundly my life, and the lives of those I mentor, have changed through this practice.

Examples of emotions and sensations which you absorb from others, or possess yourself, which can be loved include:

- Boredom
- Guilt
- Frustration
- Fatigue
- Apathy
- Disappointment
- Hopelessness

239

- Grief
- Anger
- Disgust
- Embarrassment
- Greed
- Anxiety
- Loneliness
- Hostility
- Intimidation
- Painful sensations
- Self-loathing thoughts

And the list could go on. What you read above is only a taste of the possible emotions, thoughts, and sensations that can be embraced with unconditional love.

The question now is, how to go about loving all that arises? The most vital element of unconditional love is awareness. Without being conscious of what you're experiencing, you will react blindly. In order to become aware, you need to slow down your mind and be alert. One of the best ways to become more self-aware is through meditation and mindfulness. If you're not familiar with meditation, it is basically the practice of calming the mind and being aware. Mindfulness on the other hand, is about paying close attention to the present moment. Coupled together, mindfulness and meditation will help you to notice energy vampires, foreign emotional energy, and the moments when you're emotionally triggered. Once you've noticed the feelings and sensations within you, you can then compassionately allow the emotions to be just as they are.

From what I have observed, most empaths who try mindfulness and meditation struggle to allow the emotions to just be within them, without attaching to them. We're so used to getting caught up in the dramatic stories of other's emotional energy, that it can be tough to witness without identification. Remember, even failing to love whatever arises is an opportunity to love. Love the frustration and anger, let those feelings be there within you, honor them. Remind yourself that you are not these emotions, and allow them to naturally dissolve.

Loving whatever arises takes loyal commitment; it is not a quick fix. But it is the best long-term solution out there that I know of and support.

By taking self-responsibility, sending back energy, setting boundaries, using emotional discernment, cutting ties with toxic people, and practicing self-love, you will be able to find inner emotional balance and freedom. The joy and utter freedom I have seen other people experience (including myself) from these practices is immense and truly beyond words.

Chapter 17 – Flowing With Spirit

*"Compassion hurts. When you feel connected to everything, you also feel responsible for everything. And you cannot turn away. Your destiny is bound with the destinies of others. You must either learn to carry the Universe or be crushed by it. You must grow strong enough to love the world, yet empty enough to sit down at the same table with its worst horrors." – **Andrew Boyd**

As empaths, we have one foot in this world, and one in the unseen world. Our delicate and finely-tuned ability to pick up on the endless energy frequencies around us is what endows us with the sacred gifts of insight, compassion, and loving-kindness. Because we feel life so intensely, we feel the most at peace when our hearts are open and balanced. It is in our nature to nurture, help, and give to others.

It is so important for us as empaths to maintain a sense of compassionate connectedness with life. When we put up walls to protect ourselves, we end up exhausting, victimizing, and alienating ourselves. It is far more satisfying, effective, and healthy to work with our gifts, rather than against them. Our natural tendency as empaths, and in fact, as human beings, is to be *open* to existence. Whenever we resist, block, or shield ourselves from life, we experience great repercussions in the form of mental, physical, and spiritual illnesses.

As mentioned earlier in this book, we are often misled to believe that creating healthy boundaries means "cloaking" and "shielding" ourselves from life. But as we explored, "cloaking" and "shielding" techniques are not sustainable practices. While such techniques can be practiced for short term relief, they do not help us to face life in a healthy and empowered way in the long term.

Just think about this: how long can you hold your arms outwards in an attempt to block another person? Creating cloaks, walls, and energy "bubbles" works on the exact same premise. Resisting other's energy gets very exhausting, very quickly! Not only that, but because we can't choose what energy we block out, we also tend to block out positive energy. When we block out the good, we tend to block many wonderful opportunities and people who enter our lives. As one woman who wrote to me said, "I didn't realize how damaging shielding myself from others was. I was blocking the good, but also blocking the bad that was mixed in with the good. All of that 'bad/good' energy can teach me something about myself and help me to grow as a person."

Our natural tendency is to flow with life, not to constantly resist it and put up a wall against it. Instead of minimizing or hiding ourselves away, it is much healthier to learn how to "flow" with this energy. In other words, instead of being sponges, we need to learn how to be so porous that energy flows in and out of us without getting stuck.

In this chapter, you'll learn how to do just that: to flow with whatever energy comes your way as an empowered empath. Before that, we'll explore a few techniques that will help you purify and cleanse any stagnant energy in your body.

Cleansing and Purifying Energy

Have you ever gone through periods of chronic illness or extreme exhaustion? How often do you feel nervous, irritable, high-strung, down or "not like yourself"? Perhaps the only feeling you can identify within you is more of a "sensation" of darkness, heaviness, and muddiness. What about your body? Do you experience any constant aches, pains or areas of muscle tension?

All of the sensations and feelings I've just described point to the presence of negative energy within the body. In truth, there is no such thing as "negative" energy, just energy that is heavier and denser than other energy, and therefore more uncomfortable to experience. In fact, for this section we'll replace the "negative" label with the word "heavy," as it's important for us to develop an open attitude towards energy. Often, labelling energy as negative causes our minds and hearts to close, ironically generating even more heavy energy within us.

So what can we do to cleanse and purify the heavy energy within us? So far, we have explored many different techniques in this book that will help you find more inner balance. But in this section, I'll share with you some of the best practices for cleansing your energy field, subtle body or aura. By cleansing your energy field, you will be more easily able to access states of calm and inner peace as an empath.

Firstly, we'll briefly explore what the subtle body, or aura, are. "Subtle body" and "aura" are terms that refer to the various layers of vibrating energy that compose your energy field. Although we can't see these layers of energy with the human eye, we can often feel them and access them in alternate states of consciousness (such as through shamanic journeying).

All energy that we receive originates in the spiritual realm and flows down through the head (crown chakra) and into the physical body. Whenever this energy is not permitted to flow freely it creates mental, emotional, and physical disturbances within us. As such, whatever cleansing we do at the auric level will influence our entire being.

Other than seeing an energy worker, here are some "homemade" cleansing and purifying remedies for your subtle body:

1. Smudging

Smudging is a Native American practice which traditionally uses white sage to cleanse heavy energy. But you don't need to only use white sage; other common herbs such as rosemary, lavender, sweetgrass, juniper, and mugwort are perfect choices. Smudging is performed by burning a smudge stick, which is composed of bundled together leaves and herbs. All you need to make a smudge stick is string, herbs, matches, and a bowl of sand to put out the smudge stick. Light the tip of the smudge stick and draw the smoke over your head and around your body. Ensure you have a small bowl of sand underneath the stick to catch any embers. Once you are finished, snub out the smudge stick in the bowl of sand.

2. Do a daily energy cleansing ceremony

Make a ritual of cleansing your energy. Light a candle and ask the flame to help you burn away any self-destructive patterns or energy from others that is stuck. Imagine breathing the fire into your being and visualize it clearing away the dense and dark blockages.

3. Epsom salt bath

Epsom salts help the physical body flush out toxins and the subtle body shed layers of energy debris. Simply add one cup of epsom salts to warm water, and rest in the water for twenty minutes. Epsom salts are commonly used to relieve muscle tension and also provide the body with a good source of magnesium.

4. Swim in the ocean

The energy, minerals, and salt of the ocean are extremely cleansing to your energy field. Even simply sitting by the ocean will infuse your body with negative ions, which are molecules that enhance your mood, stimulate energy, and refresh your entire energy field.

5. Expose yourself to the elements

Sunshine, wind, rain, fire, and earth are all immensely grounding to the body. Whenever you get the chance, allow yourself to feel these elements. Nature helps to cleanse the auric field and recenter the body.

6. Drink fresh water

Drinking plenty of water is an easy way to cleanse your energy field. Try drinking filtered or spring water, if possible – the cleaner, the better. Aim to drink eight or more cups of water a day.

7. Visualize healing white light

Light (whether real or imagined) is a classic way to cleanse your energy field. Start your visualization by sitting or lying down. Breathe deeply and allow your body to relax for a few minutes. As you breathe deeply, visualize a soft white light filling your body. Visualize this soft light dissolving any blockages or energy that no longer serves you. Imagine the light soaking into your head, face, neck, chest, arms, torso, legs, and feet. Give yourself space to enjoy the feeling of the white light cleansing your energy field.

Chakra Balancing

According to ancient Indian thought, our chakras are swirling "wheels" of energy within our bodies that play an integral role in our well-being. There are seven chakras in total, and they start at the base of the spine and move all the way up to the crown of the head.

You might not realize it, but as an empath, the health of your chakras plays a vital role in how strong and healthy you feel every day. When any of your chakras are imbalanced or blocked, you will feel a number of consequences ranging from physical ailments to unhappy relationships with others and even serious mental illnesses. As energy-sensitive people, taking care of our chakras should be a priority. Thankfully, all of the advice in this book so far will help you to cleanse, harmonize, and balance your energy in one way or another. However, there are a few other chakra-specific visualizations you might like to practice to help you purge any stagnant energy stuck in your energy field.

Here is a quick an easy guide to the seven chakras so you can practice the visualizations below effortlessly:

- **Root Chakra** is associated with the color red, connected to the genitals, and is ruled by the element of earth. Purpose: instinct, survival, and safety.
- **Sacral Chakra** is associated with the color orange, connected to the pelvis, and is ruled by the element of water. Purpose: passion, pleasure, and sensuality.
- **Solar Plexus Chakra** is associated with the color yellow, connected to the abdomen, and is ruled by the element of fire. Purpose: action, intention, and identity.
- **Heart Chakra** is associated with the color green, connected to the chest, and is ruled by the element of air. Purpose: self-love, compassion, and openness.
- **Throat Chakra** is associated with the color blue, connected to the throat, and is ruled by the element of ether. Purpose: authenticity, creativity, and understanding.
- **Third Eye Chakra** is associated with the color indigo, connected to the brow, and is ruled by the element of light. Purpose: insight and wisdom.
- **Crown Chakra** is associated with the color violet, connected to the top of the head, and is ruled by the element of thought. Purpose: unity, self-realization, and enlightenment.

Here are four different ways to cleanse and open your chakras. Don't worry about practicing them all straight away. Simply find one that works for you:

1. Flush energy into the earth.

Imagine a pure stream of water running through the top of your head all the way to the bottom of your feet. As this pure water runs vertically through your body, imagine it picking up all of the dirt and debris lodged within your chakras. Visualize this dirt being flushed into the earth. Notice how you start to feel clear and more energized inside. This practice usually takes about four to six minutes (although everyone's different).

2. Grounding your chakras.

The grounding visualization is useful for all chakra work as it helps you to find balance while working with your subtle energy. In order to ground your chakras, simply imagine that your body is a tree; perhaps a fir or oak tree. Visualize your feet as roots that pull up energy from the earth into your body. Feel your energy start to become solid and balanced. This practice works particularly well out in nature. Try this practice for three minutes or more.

3. Breathe in spaciousness.

Breathe gently and calmly, and focus on one particular chakra that you would like to open. For example, if you want to work with your solar plexus, focus on your abdomen and bring empty spaciousness into that area. Feel all the knots and kinks loosen as you fill this area with air. Enjoy the feeling of spaciousness opening your chakras. Continue this practice for three to five minutes.

4. Color cleansing.

Visualize a bright luminescent ball of color swirling within your chakras. Make sure that the color you choose corresponds to the chakra you intend to work with, e.g. choose a red ball of light for your root chakra, a green ball of light for your heart chakra, and so forth. Imagine the swirling vortex of light dissolving all of the deeply lodged pain and tension within you. You might like to work methodically from your root chakra all the way to your crown chakra or just focus on one problem area. For instance, if you're struggling with feeling unheard, you might like to focus on your throat chakra. Think about what issue you're struggling with and locate the corresponding chakra. Color cleansing can take between four to six minutes, but you might like to extend this visualization to ten minutes if you're feeling particularly blocked.

These four simple visualizations will help reinstate vitality and balance within your body and energy field. You might like to use these visualizations as supplements which assist you in carrying out the most important practice explored in this chapter: SOAR.

What is SOAR?

SOAR stands for Surrender, Observe, Allow, and Release. Interestingly, the word "soar" nicely doubles to mean "to fly or transcend." In other words, this practice was created by the two of us to help you soar far above the darkness and emotional congestion that you experience as an empath. Designed specifically for empaths struggling with engulfing emotions such as stress, anxiety, and depression, SOAR has been lovingly inspired by mindfulness based stress reduction (MBSR), zen philosophy, and self-inquiry.

SOAR is, at its core, a way of life. This practice is not just a slap-and-dash technique that can be plastered over pain: SOAR goes to the very root of the suffering we experience as empaths and is the most powerful practice recommended in this book. When practiced consistently, SOAR will help you to experience profound mental, emotional, and spiritual freedom. However, this practice does require a bit of effort, patience, and dedication!

The wonderful thing about SOAR is that it can help you overcome every obstacle that you face as an empath, namely:

- Internalizing emotional energy
- Attaching to emotional energy, and
- Suffering as a result of attaching to this emotional energy

Here is how SOAR can be broken down:

Surrender is about consciously relaxing your body by simply noticing your breath and allowing yourself to feel the energy within you.

Observation is about making the energy within you tangible by giving it a name, shape, size, smell, etc. This step is about developing an open, curious, and non-judgmental attitude towards whatever you're experiencing. By observing the emotions and sensations within you, you will stop mentally identifying with them – this is called "non-attachment" and adopting the role of the "witnesser."

Allowing is about embracing the emotions and sensations within you just as they are. Allowing is really about being unconditionally open or loving towards how you feel, without identifying with or attaching to the feelings.

Release is about allowing the emotions and sensations to naturally fade away or dissipate as you observe and allow them. Releasing also involves letting go of the mental stories and thoughts that create our pain so that we can experience freedom from suffering.

As the famous quote by psychiatrist Carl Jung goes, "What you resist not only persists, but will grow in size." Therefore, the more we resist what we feel as empaths, the more we suffer. But the more we openly face the painful and congested emotional energy within us, the more opportunity we have to release these sensations.

How to Practice SOAR

Like any powerful technique, SOAR should be practiced and mastered little by little, kind of like meditation. You won't be great at it right away, and you might even feel frustrated by the practice at first. But even your frustration and annoyance is an opportunity to practice SOAR! Any emotion that comes from both within you, and without you, can be used with SOAR.

Try setting aside a few minutes each day to familiarize yourself with this practice. For example, you might like to dedicate ten minutes in the morning to practicing SOAR or use time during your lunch break or afternoon commute to practice. Gradually, as you get more skilled at this practice, you'll find yourself wanting to use SOAR more and more. In this case, you can gradually increase the amount of time you use SOAR until it becomes a living and breathing lifestyle rather than just a practice.

One fun approach to SOAR is to pick any moment or situation in your day that generates anxiety, tension, fatigue or inner heaviness.

Here is an example:

You're feeling sick and anxious today. So many people are walking around you, talking loudly, laughing, gossiping, demanding, and brimming with nervous vibes. You realize that you're starting to feel dizzy and overwhelmed by the energy around you. Taking a break, you decide to connect with your breath. As you gently notice your breath, you sense that the nervous feeling of dizziness within you is in your head. This feeling looks and feels like a black tornado spinning around. As you observe the sensation, you sit with it and allow it to play out. Continuing to stay grounded with your breath, you notice fearful thoughts arising, but you let them go. Gradually the dizzy anxiety begins to release naturally.

Here is another example of SOAR broken down:

Surrender: You've just spoken to a needy and high-strung friend, but you seem to have absorbed some of their energy. Dropping into your breath, you decide to connect with your body. By anchoring yourself to your breath, you're able to discover nervous tension building in your neck.

Observe: You explore this feeling, and it seems to feel jagged and cold, kind of like razor wire.

Allow: Continuing to stay present with your breath, you allow this sensation to be present in your body, exactly as it is, without wanting or needing it to change.

Release: The more you are present with this sensation without identifying with it or claiming it as your own, the more you feel it fade. Gently, you observe any thoughts that arise, and continue allowing the feelings within you. Finally, you start to feel more relaxed and grounded as the energy starts releasing by itself.

The goal of SOAR is to help you become so open that it is impossible for any emotion or sensation, whether within or without you, to become "stuck." The more porous and open you can be, the more energy will flow in and out of you, unhindered. And the more energy can flow freely, the more light, energized, grounded, and empowered you will feel.

The Importance of Individuation

As mentioned earlier in this book, it is vital for all empaths to complete the process of Individuation; of becoming fully matured human beings. As we explored in chapter 16, completing this Individuation process involves practicing self-responsibility, self-love, emotional discernment, and the setting of clear boundaries. Without undergoing this process of psychological and emotional growth, we begin confusing other's emotions as our own, setting poor boundaries, sacrificing our needs, attracting narcissists and energy vampires, and falling into toxic behavioral patterns.

While SOAR can be practiced at any point or stage in life, we recommend using it in conjunction with the process of Individuation. Before opening yourself through the practice of SOAR, it is best to develop a strong sense of self with clearly defined boundaries. Without these strong boundaries, SOAR will fail to offer you the relief you're searching for. You need to be able to ground your consciousness in your body before you practice SOAR. If your attention and energy is scattered everywhere, you will find it almost impossible to carry out this practice. Therefore, if you find yourself still working to create a clear Individuated sense of self, try to focus on the other

254

practices mentioned in this book before committing to SOAR. Thankfully, we've written and structured this book in a way that will apply to you at any stage of your empath journey. So if you're a beginner, start at the beginning of the book; if you've already started your spiritual journey, focus more on the middle of this book. If you've done a lot of soulwork, focus on this chapter.

Even if you're a beginner, you will benefit from many of the practices already mentioned in this chapter. Familiarizing yourself with SOAR will help you to know what to work towards.

Step-by-Step Guide to SOAR

To help you actively practice SOAR, I've broken down the process step-by-step below. You'll also read a few real life examples to help you understand the steps better.

Surrender

Surrender is about letting go of resistance to what you feel. Usually as empaths we tend to fight, resist, condemn or avoid what we're feeling because it's simply too overwhelming. It seems almost counterintuitive to "surrender" to what we feel, but the very act of surrender is the beginning process of experiencing peace. When we can move through life without resistance to what we feel inside and sense from others, we experience profound levels of freedom. Suddenly, nothing can truly hurt or harm us because emotional energy is seen for what it truly is: just energy!

In order to surrender and meet whatever you're experiencing, try to focus on your breathing. You don't need to force yourself to breathe in any special way (although deep breathing does help); simply relax into your breath, no matter how fast, shallow, deep or slow it is. To start practicing SOAR, mentally drop into your body and notice your breath. Relax into your breath as it goes in and out. Sometimes, simply connecting to your breath is enough to reinstate feelings of wellbeing again. Surrender into whatever breathing rhythm you're most comfortable with. You don't need to force anything. There are no rules here! However, if you need a bit of help, try counting four seconds as you breathe in, four seconds as you pause, and four seconds as you breathe out.

Remember that there's no need to force yourself to breathe in any special way, because often this creates even more underlying anxiety and tension. However, if you're on the verge of panic, you might like to gently focus on breathing from your stomach as this will help to calm down your body. But once again, deep breathing is not essential. Find your own natural rhythm and concentrate on your breath, on the in and out breath. This stage is about surrendering thoughts and allowing your attention to melt into the breath. Once you have steadily connected with your breath, you can continue.

Observe

Ensuring that you are grounded through your breath, allow yourself to locate the feelings within you. Where are the feelings or sensations physically located in your body? Become curious. What do they look like, sound like, smell like, feel like, even taste like? Try giving the emotional energy in your body a shape, texture, temperature or color. The more tangible you can make the sensations within you, the more you will be able to practice non-attachment. Non-attachment or disidentification is important because it helps you to treat the sensations within you objectively. Instead of believing that these sensations are "yours" or mean something terrible about you, non-attachment helps you to understand such feelings as simply energy.

For example, you might identify anxiety within your chest and observe it to feel like explosive fireworks constantly startling you. You might witness the anger pulsating within you like a red hot boil. You might walk into a room and notice how the clashing energy feels like a whirlpool in your chest or two walls tightly compressing your body. Even if you can't identify an emotion, you can still observe what the sensation within you feels like, and where it is located. For instance, you might notice that around a certain person you always feel uncomfortable, even creeped out. You might notice that the energy you're absorbing from this person feels dense and dark, like a ton of slime deposited in your heart area.

The different ways that you observe the energy within you will always be unique to the context you're experiencing. Remember to stay connected to your breath and to maintain an open and curious attitude about what you're feeling or sensing. Remaining open to difficult emotions can be hard, so don't expect to be perfect at this step straight away. Almost everyone struggles with this step at first.

Here are some examples of different emotions and how they may feel in your body while observing them:

Fear – a black suffocating cloak over your whole body
Frustration – hot tingling in your throat
Sadness – a heavy, wet puddle in your chest
Jealousy – shards of cold glass in your head
Shame – the feeling or image of falling off a cliff

257

Despair – a fist squeezing your heart
Insecurity – grey zigzag patterns in your head and chest
Hatred – boiling lava in your brain
Lust – a ravenous black dog in your stomach
Panic – alarm bells jumping up and down within you
Depression – a numbing grey fog in your heart area
Anxiety – black spiders crawling up your spine

By witnessing these emotions, you will be giving them the chance to be seen and acknowledged, without burying them away.

Allow

Our knee-jerk response to heavy energy is to reject it immediately. We reject heavy energy by shaming, outlawing, and demonizing it. We talk of "banishing," "removing," and "getting rid" of heavy energy. But ironically, by rejecting this energy, we perpetuate even more fear and intolerance towards life.

The only alternative to rejecting painful energy is allowing or accepting it. By acceptance, I don't mean adopting a defeatist mindset. Allowing is about embracing whatever arises within you, no matter how bad it feels. In essence, allowing is a form of unconditional love because it is completely accepting of whatever type of emotions arise.

Allowing is also about realizing that whatever emotional energy you're experiencing is temporary. All emotions are like visitors which come and eventually go. The more you resist these emotions, the more they hang around you. In fact, resisting, identifying with, and suppressing emotions is the number one reason why we become so sick and overwhelmed

258

as empaths. But the more embracing and accommodating you are towards the emotions you feel, without identifying with them, the more quickly they leave.

Staying connected to your breath, allow whatever feelings arise just the way they are without wanting or needing them to change. Realize that everything passes and changes, including what you're experiencing. Give the sensations within you the opportunity to be witnessed and acknowledged.

Release

As you go through the gentle process of surrendering, observing, and allowing the emotional energy within you, you will eventually sense a shift within you. Gradually (sometimes very quickly) the heavy emotional energy within you will begin to disintegrate and gently fade away. You might experience this shift as a release of inner tension, a sensation of inner spaciousness or a feeling of peace entering you. Releasing is also about letting go of the intrusive thoughts that enter our minds which perpetuate our suffering. By learning how to release emotionally-charged thoughts by simply allowing whatever we feel, we become compassionate towards our suffering. This self-compassion, in turn, helps us to find peace again.

Applying SOAR

If you're interested in trying SOAR for yourself, try to set aside a regular time or period each day. For example, you might like to reserve five or ten minutes in the morning or evenings.

To help you actively apply SOAR to your life, we have recorded a free guided audio with this eBook which you can

259

find on our website (https://lonerwolf.com/soar/). You'll also find a free downloadable poster with the steps laid out clearly.

For now, here's SOAR put into practice again, this time, with a common situation so many empaths have shared with me:

You've just come home from working a ten hour shift. You've been around tense and angry people all day and you're feeling frazzled and on edge. Instead of ignoring or distracting yourself from these emotions, you decide to take a shower and connect with your breath. Focusing on your breathing for a few minutes, you explore where the feeling of anxiety appear in your body. You discover that there is a pulling sensation in your chest where the anxiety is located. This pulling sensation looks like a rope tugging at your heart that's about to snap. Continuing to focus on your breathing, you become completely present with this sensation. You allow yourself to experience the tugging sensation fully, accepting it just as it is. As thoughts creep into your mind, you allow them too, letting go of your attachment to them. As you allow all sensations and thoughts to play out in your body for a few minutes, you begin to feel the tugging pull of anxiety lessen, until it has altogether disappeared.

Remember, SOAR can be applied to *any* feeling or sensation you experience, no matter how painful or disturbing. Whenever any emotion is met with conscious acceptance and non-attachment, you will find that it quickly passes away.

Finding Peace Within the Storm

Try to experiment with SOAR for one week. Be patient. This technique requires dedication. It can take a while to master this practice, so enjoy the journey. There are a hell of a lot of opportunities to practice SOAR out there! Also, don't forget to check out the free guided SOAR meditations if you need extra help (https://lonerwolf.com/soar/).

If you have any questions about SOAR, you might also like to refer to the Appendix section at the end of this book for some helpful troubleshooting tips. These tips will help you get through sticky areas (such as raging thoughts) and bring more inner clarity.

As we've explored in this chapter, the number one reason why we suffer as empaths is because we have the habit of unconsciously resisting and attaching to everything that we absorb. By regularly applying SOAR to your life, you can find peace even in the middle of the most stressful, intense, and overwhelming circumstances.

May you find peace within the storm.

Chapter 18 – The Spiritual Purpose of Empaths

*"Being an empath is so ... beautiful. When you're in whole alignment with yourself and higher purpose, life becomes a beautiful fireworks display." – **Tabitha, empath reader from lonerwolf.com***

As an empath, you were born into this world as a wild and completely unique expression of the Divine. Whether you believe in a Higher Power or not, deep down you have always sensed that there is more to life than meets the eye. How often have you seen or felt that which others don't notice? How often have you had experiences that defy all understanding?

At this time in history, we are in need of sensitivity more than ever. While that statement may sound outrageous, the truth is that the more obsessed be become with externality, the more impoverished we become inside of ourselves. The more we stay focused on money, fame, status, power, beauty, and other external pursuits, the more distant we become from our Souls. The more distant we become from our Souls, the more we suffer as a society from what is known as "Soul Loss."

Soul Loss is a shamanic term which points to a state of being in which we have completely lost contact with our Souls. While our Souls are always here within us, we can easily sever our contact with them through shallow and ego-centered living. Have you ever heard someone use the expression "it has lost its Soul?" When we use this expression what we're really saying is that something or someone has lost touch with authentic, heart-centered expression. The same can be said for our society: it has lost its Soul.

The deeply nourishing values of love, compassion, empathy, humility, reverence, receptivity, tolerance, interconnectedness, and sensitivity have been replaced with words such as profitability, progress, reputation, accomplishment, industriousness, practicality, and stardom. While there is nothing wrong with these new values, they have created a warped and imbalanced society that focuses solely on the external pursuit of success.

The moment we value the external over the internal is the moment we lose touch with our deepest selves. As empaths, we understand this on an intuitive level. Perhaps our global Soul Loss is precisely why we feel so "alien" and displaced on this planet in the first place? With so much fear, isolation, rage, and grief pulsating in the people around us, it's no wonder that we feel perpetually weighed down.

All I can say is *thank God we exist.* That may sound like an ironic statement, but think for a moment ... what would this planet be like without sensitive and empathic people? Can you imagine the level of emotional desolation there would be? Can you imagine how deeply disturbed and stunted the human race would be (more than it currently is) without sensitive people? Perhaps you don't want to imagine; the thought is quite depressing.

If you don't feel like you belong here, that is completely understandable. Living in a soulless society can be hard. In fact, "hard" is an understatement. Living in a soulless society can be completely isolating, overwhelming, and often tortuous. We feel deeper, more intensely, and more persistently than those around us. We even feel what *other* people are afraid to feel within themselves. But it is this very ability to feel deeply and be so receptive to others that is our greatest strength. Yes, this strength can also be our greatest weakness when we don't know how to ground and harness it, but it is the planet's saving grace.

Now, more than ever, our society is in need of sensitive and empathic people. Now, more than ever, the human race needs to go inwards and connect with the Soul again. As natural born healers, intuitives, and mentors, it is not only our responsibility, but also our destiny to help humanity heal.

How You Can Use Your Gift to Change the World

The good news is that by reading this book, you have already taken the first step in transforming this planet. In some way, whatever you learn and translate into action thanks to this book will be passed on to others around you. Through time, your growth will inspire others around you in ways you can't possibly fathom. It is truly amazing how committing to the spiritual path of growth can have a ripple effect for many generations to come.

When all has been said and done, the way you choose to use your gift is completely up to you and your unique strengths and preferences. However, if you're interested in a little more guidance, I recommend that you start with the practices mentioned in this book. Start by implementing the advice mentioned in the physical healing chapter, and work your way through to the mental, emotional, and spiritual healing chapters. By choosing to take care of yourself, you will naturally take care of others. By caring for yourself and others, you will fulfill the mission of every empath: to help humanity heal. The best place to start is with yourself!

Often, using our gift as empaths naturally translates to finding a job that reflects our deepest wishes. For example, you may focus on inspiring people through your artwork, helping others recover from addiction as a psychologist, aiding people in relaxing through massage therapy, or even supporting the rights of underprivileged children. There are countless tasks, roles, and professions you can adopt as an empath. But the question is, how can you find your meaning in life; something that will truly fulfil you?

Here are a few recommendations:

1. Brainstorm on a piece of paper everything that invigorates you and connect the dots.
2. Think back to what you enjoyed doing as a child.
3. Explore what you enjoy doing in your spare time or as a hobby.
4. List all of your strengths and reflect on them. Ask others for help if you find it hard to list your strengths.
5. Write your own personal mission statement, i.e. what would you like to specifically offer the world or actually have written on your gravestone?
6. Ask your Soul for guidance in the form of a prayer.
7. Ask yourself, "How can I best give my gift away to others?" Whatever answer makes you want to cry with joy is your meaning in life.

Repeat these recommendations until something bursts into your awareness and takes your breath away.

By slowly and steadily implementing the advice mentioned in this book, you will not only become calm, centered, grounded, empowered, and unconditionally loving towards yourself, but you will also be fulfilling your spiritual destiny. It takes only one person to change the world, and that person is you.

What to Do Now

Now that you have reached the end of this book, you may be wondering what to do next. You have explored many powerful techniques that will help you create calmness and inner balance on the physical, emotional, mental, and spiritual levels. You have learned about your Shadow Self, how to handle narcissists and energy vampires, and how to approach relationships with others. You have even explored the spiritual awakening process and how you can use your empathic gift to change the world. But with all this knowledge, where do you start?

The best place to start making deep changes in your life is to observe where you currently are. Ask yourself, what are your greatest needs in this moment as an empath? If you're struggling with physical problems such as chronic illness and pain, start with the physical realm chapter. If you're suffering from low self-worth and problems such as anxiety and depression, focus on the mental realm chapter. If you're feeling overwhelmed in your relationships with others, start with the emotional realm chapter. Finally, if you just need to feel more grounded and centered, work with the spiritual realm chapter.

The Importance of Community

You don't need to travel your journey alone as an empath. As a sensitive person, you thrive the best when you're surrounded by a nurturing group of people. As one woman wrote on our blog, "It has taken me a long time to realize I'm not broken, or weak, or crazy for feeling the way I do, and knowing there are others out there that struggle with the same issues is comforting."

To help you access more guidance, we have created a caring and safe community where you can share your thoughts, concerns, and struggles with others. Join our community by going to: www.facebook.com/groups/AwakenedEmpath/.

Alternatively, you might like to create your own real life empath support group. Having the support of others who share your gift will help you to feel encouraged, inspired, and affirmed. It is immensely nourishing to have the presence of other sensitive people in our lives.

Here is some advice on how to create your own empath support or study group:

- **Type.** What type of group will you have: online or in-the-flesh?
- **Location.** Where will you meet together as a group? Try to think of quiet places such as in the library, park or in a private home.
- **Membership.** Will your group be open to the public or open only by invitation?
- **Length and frequency.** Decide how long you will meet together for, e.g. one hour, and how often, e.g. weekly, bimonthly or monthly.
- **Size.** How big do you want your group to be? For example, you may prefer a small group of between three and five people. On the other hand, you might like to create a large group of fifty or more people.
- **Objective.** What will be the objective or purpose of your group? You might like to write a mission

statement such as, "Our mission is to create a safe space in which Empaths can thrive and find support."

- **Recommended reading.** Choose various chapters of this book to discuss and explore with each other. For example, you might like to pass this book around your group and read three pages each. Start with the beginning of the book, and progress all the way through to the end together.
- **Format and structure.** Think about how you would like to structure your group meetings. Choose a new leader of the group each month and think about whether the group will be open to informal discussion. Often, it's better to take a structured approach to creating a group to avoid it turning into a pity party.

You might also like to incorporate other practices into your group such as meditation, SOAR practice or deep breathing. Don't forget to check out our free SOAR guided meditation on our website (https://lonerwolf.com/soar/).

Final Words

You are a being of immense depth, wisdom, and compassion. You are a pioneer and trailblazer of humanity, a model for others on how to be sensitive and powerful. All the strength and love you need is already within you, waiting to be discovered.

Reflect on all the changes that have happened in your life since reading this book: what subtle or significant shifts have you begun to experience? By slowly and steadily implementing the advice mentioned in this book, you will not only become calm, grounded, empowered, and unconditionally loving towards yourself, but you will also be fulfilling your destiny. It takes only one person to change the world, and that person is you.

Create boundaries. Honor your limits. Say no. Take a break. Let go. Stay grounded. Nurture your body. Love your vulnerability. And if all else fails, breathe deeply.

Finally, remember that true strength lies not in sheltering yourself from the world, but learning how to stay grounded and open. Balance is the key here.

May the wisdom that you've gleaned from this book continue to uplift, educate, and inspire you on your sacred journey as an empath. You are beautiful, sacred, and perfect just as you are. Be blessed.

Appendix

Troubleshooting SOAR

SOAR takes time and effort to practice and apply to your life. As empaths, we tend to have a large number of conditioned and ingrained habits that often take years to reprogram, so don't expect to be a Zen master over night!

To make your SOAR practice as effective as possible, here are a few of the most common questions and issues that arise.

Q. I keep forgetting the steps of SOAR. What do I do?

SOAR is designed to be a process, not a rigid step-by-step formula. Nevertheless, remembering the steps does help you to to practice it in the beginning. If you can't remember each of words (Surrender, Observe, Allow, Release), try to attach an image or story to each of the steps. For example, you might image a person sitting down, breathing deeply, and different parts of their body lighting up with emotion.

Q. I can't seem to focus on my breath.

It can be difficult to focus on the breath when the mind is tense and full of raging thoughts. Instead of strenuously trying to ground yourself with your breath, it helps to relax your focus. Focusing on your breath can be compared to watching the TV; it doesn't and shouldn't require a lot of arduous effort. Therefore, try to approach breathing with the same quality of awareness that you approach watching the television. Also, remember that you don't need to force yourself to breathe deeply if it doesn't come naturally to you at first. After a few minutes, your breathing might naturally deepen, but the point is not to control your breathing, but rather, to surrender or relax into it.

Q. I can't seem to release an emotion.

The goal of SOAR is not to forcefully release an emotion. Instead, releasing emotional energy is a byproduct of observing and allowing whatever arises within you. If you're struggling to release emotional energy, you probably aren't completely allowing the feelings. Don't worry. Your resistance to the way you're feeling is something to also apply SOAR to! Focus on your breathing and locate the resistance in your body. Then, embrace it, exactly as it is. Sometimes certain emotions can't be completely released straight away because they have been buried for too long. If this is the case, simply release as much as you can, and return to the sensation at a later time.

Q. I can't locate the emotion in my body.

Try to bring your attention to your breath for a few minutes. A frantic mind struggles to locate and observe emotions. Focus on your breathing and then try again.

Q. I keep identifying with the emotional energy and struggle with non-attachment. What can help?

It is completely normal to forget that the energy within you is just energy, and quickly get wound up in identifying with it. Often, it can take a bit of practice to objectively observe and allow the emotion within you, particularly if it is an intense feeling such as anger or fear. Simply return back to your breath for a few moments so that you become grounded again. Then, start the process again of observing, allowing, and releasing.

Q. After I finish SOAR, the sensation returns again. What can I do?

Intense and jammed away emotions have a tendency to come back. SOAR helps these suppressed emotions to bubble to the surface, so often you will need to return to the start again. Go through each of the steps as many times as you need. Remember pain is often like an onion with many layers: be patient and give yourself time to peel back every layer. Sometimes, certain types of deeply buried pain (like repressed grief) need to be revisited over and over again. Be patient and give yourself as much time as you need.

Q. I keep experiencing heavy and oppressive energy from others. What next?

It is the nature of life to experience all types of energy. SOAR isn't about preventing you from experiencing this energy, it is about helping you to release it so that it doesn't get stuck in your energy field. Whenever you feel yourself beginning to suffer from other people's energy, take a few moments to focus on your breathing and apply SOAR. With practice, SOAR can be applied in any moment or situation when you're feeling burdened by the energy around you.

Q. I'm experiencing multiple emotions and sensations at once. I can't focus on all of them.

If you feel absolutely bombarded by many different types of emotional energy, try to focus on only one area of your body to apply SOAR, e.g. your head area. After you have released the

273

energy in your head area, move onto different parts of your body which many be storing energy such as your neck, chest or stomach. Apply SOAR separately to each of these places. Alternatively, simply rest in your breath for a while. Often surrendering into the breath helps the body to calm down.

Q. My thoughts are consuming me. What can I do about this?

Getting sucked into thought streams is completely normal. We're so used to living in the mind that becoming conscious of our thoughts can be very difficult at first. Try to approach your mind in the same way as you would watching a YouTube video or TV program: be curious. Think of your mind as a television channel and observe how fleeting your thoughts are. Notice how emotionally-charged they can be and don't fight them. Resisting your thoughts, attempting to "control" them or "trying not to think" only gives your thoughts more power! Simply allow your thoughts by observing them. Noticing your thoughts doesn't need to be hard: it's just like watching TV! However, if you absolutely can't do this, then keep returning back to your breath.

Q. SOAR doesn't work no matter what I do.

The biggest block to experiencing emotional release from SOAR is your expectations. When you expect this practice to be an instant "cure-all" you create resistance to the process. Try to examine your mindset: are you putting too much pressure on not only this practice, but yourself? This practice is simply about learning how to be present with your pain. Let go of the outcome and focus on the process. Release only comes as a natural product of allowing energy to move through you.

Did You Like Awakened Empath?

Thank you so much for purchasing Awakened Empath. We're honored that you have chosen our book to help you understand your empathic gifts. We truly hope you've enjoyed this book and now have a wide variety of practices to apply to your life.

We would like to ask you for a small favor. Would you please take just a minute to leave a review for this book on Amazon or Goodreads? This feedback will help us continue to write the kind of books that will best help you and others grow. If you really loved this book, please let us know!

Connect With Us On Social Media

If you're on Facebook, Twitter, Pinterest or Instagram, share your thoughts and feelings with us by using the hashtag #awakenedempath.

If you haven't already joined our Empath group on Facebook, go to https://www.facebook.com/groups/AwakenedEmpath/.

References

Introduction

1. Elaine N. Aron, *The Highly Sensitive Person: How to Thrive When the World Overwhelms You* (New York: Broadway Books, 1996). https://www.amazon.com/Highly-Sensitive-Person-Thrive-Overwhelms/dp/0553062182/
2. Caroline van Kimmenade, "Being Empathic versus Being an Empath: Crucial Differences," http://thehappysensitive.com/being-empathic-versus-being-empath-crucial-differences/, (August 20, 2013).

Chapter 1

1. Charles Grau et al., "Conscious Brain-to-Brain Communication in Humans Using Non-Invasive Techniques," *PLoS ONE* 9, no. 8 (2014): e105225. https://doi.org/10.1371/journal.pone.0105225. http://journals.plos.org/plosone/article?id=10.1371/journal.pone.0105225
2. https://lonerwolf.com/intuitive-empath-test/

Chapter 4

1. World Health Organization. 11-14 October 1994. "Global Strategy on Occupational Health for All: The Way to Health at Work." *Second Meeting of the WHO Collaborating Centres in Occupational Health.* Beijing, China.

http://www.who.int/occupational_health/publications/glo
bstrategy/en/index2.html

Chapter 5

1. Schoenewolf, Gerald. "Emotional Contagion: Behavioral induction in individuals and groups." Modern Psychoanalysis 15.1 (1990): 49-61.
2. Meltzoff, A N, and M K Moore. "Newborn infants imitate adult facial gestures." Child Development 54.3 (1983): 702-709.
3. Barsade, Sigal G. 2002. "The Ripple Effect: Emotional Contagion and Its Influence on Group Behavior." *Administrative Science Quarterly* 47: 644-675. http://citeseerx.ist.psu.edu/viewdoc/download?doi=10.1.1.724.7133&rep=rep1&type=pdf

Chapter 6

1. Calaprice, Alice. 2005. *The New Quotable Einstein.* Princeton, NJ: Princeton University Press, p. 206
2. Acharya, Sourya, and Samarth Shukla. 2012. "Mirror Neurons, Enigma of the Metaphysical Modular Brain." *Journal of Natural Science, Biology, and Medicine* 3 (2): 118-124. https://www.ncbi.nlm.nih.gov/pmc/articles/PMC3510904/
3. Iacoboni, Marco. 2009. *Mirroring People: The Science of Empathy and How We Connect with Others.* Picador. https://www.amazon.com/Mirroring-People-Science-Empathy-Connect/dp/0312428383
4. Ramachandran, V.S., and L.M. Oberman. 2006. "Broken Mirrors: A Theory of Autism." *Scientific*

American 295 (5): 62-9.
https://www.ncbi.nlm.nih.gov/pubmed/17076085

5. Blakemore, S. J., D. Bristow, G. Bird, J. Ward, and C. Frith. 2005. "Somatosensory Activations During the Observation of Touch and a Case of Vision-touch Synesthesia." *Brain* 128 (7): 1571-1583.

6. McDougall, W. 1927. "An Experiment for the Testing of the Hypothesis at Lamarck." *British Journal of Psychology* 17: 267.

7. Sheldrake, Rupert. 2009. *New Science of Life.* Icon Books. https://www.amazon.co.uk/New-Science-Life-Rupert-Sheldrake/dp/1848310420

8. Backster, Cleve. 1968. "Evidence of a Primary Perception in Plant Life." *International Journal of Parapsychology* 10 (4): 329-348.

9. McCraty, Rollin, Raymond Trevor Bradley, and Dana Tomasino. 2005. "The Resonant Heart." *Shift: At the Frontiers of Consciousness* 15-19. https://www.heartmath.org/research/research-library/relevant-publications/the-resonant-heart/

10. McCraty, R., M. Atkinson, and R. T. Bradley. 2004. "Electrophysiological Evidence of Intuition: Part 2. A System-Wide Process?" *Journal of Alternative Complementary Medicine* 10 (2): 325-36. https://www.ncbi.nlm.nih.gov/pubmed/15165413

11. McCraty, Rollin. 2004. "The Energetic Heart: Bioelectromagnetic Communication Within and Between People." In *Clinical Applications of Bioelectromagnetic Medicine*, by P. J. Rosch and M. S. Markov, 541-562. New York: Marcel Dekker. https://www.heartmath.org/research/research-library/energetics/energetic-heart-bioelectromagnetic-communication-within-and-between-people/

12. McCraty, Rollin, Mike Atkinson, Dana Tomasino, and William A. Tiller. 1998. "The Electricity of Touch: Detection and Measurement of Cardiac Energy Exchange Between People." In *Brain and Values: Is a Biological Science of Values Possible*, by Karl H. Pribran, 359-379. Mahwah, NJ: Lawrence Erlbaum Associates. https://www.heartmath.org/research/research-library/energetics/electricity-of-touch/

Chapter 9

1. Johnson, Robert A. 2013. *Owning Your Own Shadow: Understanding the Dark Side of Your Psyche.* HarperCollins. https://www.amazon.com/Owning-Your-Own-Shadow-Understanding-ebook/dp/B00B72CFQW/

Chapter 12

1. Aron, E. N, Aron, A., & Davies, K. M. (2005). Adult shyness: The interaction of temperamental sensitivity and an adverse childhood environment. Personality and Social Psychology Bulletin, 31, 181-197.
2. Liss, M., L. Baxley, K. Timmel, and P. Killingsworth. 2005. "Sensory Processing Sensitivity and Its Relation to Parental Bonding, Anxiety, and Depression." *Personality and Individual Differences* 39: 1429-1439.

Chapter 13

1. Campbell, Joseph. 1972. *The Hero With a Thousand Faces.* Princeton, NJ: Princeton University Press. http://www.goodreads.com/book/show/588138.The_Hero_With_a_Thousand_Faces

Chapter 14

1. McMains, S., and S. Kasner. 2011. "Interactions of Top-down and Bottom-up Mechanisms in Human Visual Cortex." *Journal of Neuroscience* 31 (2): 587-97. https://www.ncbi.nlm.nih.gov/pubmed/21228167

2. Environmental Health Association of Nova Scotia. 2004. "Cosmetics & Personal Care." *Guide to Less Toxic Products.* http://www.lesstoxicguide.ca/index.asp?fetch=personal

3. Mosin, Oleg, and Ignat Ignatov. 2013. "The Structure and Composition of Natural Corbonaceous Fullerene Containing Mineral Shungite." *International Journal of Advanced Scientific and Technical Research* 6 (3): 9-21. http://rspublication.com/ijst/dec13/2.pdf

4. Gomez-Pinilla, Fernando. 2008. "Brain Foods: The Effects of Nutrients on Brain Function." *Nature Reviews Neuroscience* 9: 568-578. http://www.nature.com/nrn/journal/v9/n7/abs/nrn2421.html

Chapter 16

1. Williamson, Marianne. 1996. *A Return to Love: Reflections on the Principles of "A Course in Miracles".* HarperOne.

Bibliography

Acharya, Sourya, and Samarth Shukla. 2012. "Mirror Neurons, Enigma of the Metaphysical Modular Brain." *Journal of Natural Science, Biology, and Medicine* 3 (2): 118-124.

Aron, E. N., A. Aron, and K. M. Davies. 2005. "Adult Shyness: The Interaction of Temperamental Sensitivity and an Adverse Childhood Environment." *Personality and Social Psychology Bulletin* 31: 181-197.

Aron, Elaine N. 1997. *The Highly Sensitive Person: How to Thrive When the World Overwhelms You.* Broadway Books.

Backster, Cleve. 1968. "Evidence of a Primary Perception in Plant Life." *International Journal of Parapsychology* 10 (4): 329-348.

Barsade, Sigal G. 2002. "The Ripple Effect: Emotional Contagion and Its Influence on Group Behavior." *Administrative Science Quarterly* 47: 644-675.

Blakemore, S. J., D. Bristow, G. Bird, J. Ward, and C. Frith. 2005. "Somatosensory Activations During the Observation of Touch and a Case of Vision-touch Synesthesia." *Brain* 128 (7): 1571-1583.

Calaprice, Alice. 2005. *The New Quotable Einstein.* Princeton, NJ: Princeton University Press.

Campbell, Joseph. 1972. *The Hero With a Thousand Faces.* Princeton, NJ: Princeton University Press.

Environmental Health Association of Nova Scotia. 2004. "Cosmetics & Personal Care." *Guide to Less Toxic Products.* http://www.lesstoxicguide.ca/index.asp?fetch=personal.

Gomez-Pinilla, Fernando. 2008. "Brain Foods: The Effects of Nutrients on Brain Function." *Nature Reviews Neuroscience* 9: 568-578.

Grau, Carles, Romauld Ginhoux, Alejandro Riera, Thanh Lam Nguyen, Hubert Chauvat, Michel Berg, Julia L. Amengual, Alvaro Pascual-Leone, and Giulio Ruffini. 2014. "Conscious Brain-to-Brain Communication in Humans Using Non-Invasive Technologies." *PLOS One.* doi:https://doi.org/10.1371/journal.pone.0105225.

Iacoboni, Marco. 2009. *Mirroring People: The Science of Empathy and How We Connect with Others.* Picador.

Johnson, Robert A. 2013. *Owning Your Own Shadow: Understanding the Dark Side of Your Psyche.* HarperCollins.

Liss, M., L. Baxley, K. Timmel, and P. Killingsworth. 2005. "Sensory Processing Sensitivity and Its Relation to Parental Bonding, Anxiety, and Depression." *Personality and Individual Differences* 39: 1429-1439.

McCraty, R., M. Atkinson, and R. T. Bradley. 2004. "Electrophysiological Evidence of Intuition: Part 2. A System-Wide Process?" *Journal of Alternative Complementary Medicine* 10 (2): 325-36.

McCraty, Rollin. 2004. "The Energetic Heart: Bioelectromagnetic Communication Within and Between

People." In *Clinical Applications of Bioelectromagnetic Medicine*, by P. J. Rosch and M. S. Markov, 541-562. New York: Marcel Dekker.

McCraty, Rollin, Mike Atkinson, Dana Tomasino, and William A. Tiller. 1998. "The Electricity of Touch: Detection and Measurement of Cardiac Energy Exchange Between People." In *Brain and Values: Is a Biological Science of Values Possible*, by Karl H. Pribran, 359-379. Mahwah, NJ: Lawrence Erlbaum Associates.

McCraty, Rollin, Raymond Trevor Bradley, and Dana Tomasino. 2005. "The Resonant Heart." *Shift: At the Frontiers of Consciousness* 15-19.

McDougall, W. 1927. "An Experiment for the Testing of the Hypothesis at Lamarck." *British Journal of Psychology* 17: 267.

McMains, S., and S. Kasner. 2011. "Interactions of Top-down and Bottom-up Mechanisms in Human Visual Cortex." *Journal of Neuroscience* 31 (2): 587-97.

Meltzoff, A. N., and M. K. Moore. 1983. "Newborn Infants Imitate Adult Facial Gestures." *Child Development* 54 (3): 702-709.

Mosin, Oleg, and Ignat Ignatov. 2013. "The Structure and Composition of Natural Corbonaceous Fullerene Containing Mineral Shungite." *International Journal of Advanced Scientific and Technical Research* 6 (3): 9-21.

Ramachandran, V.S., and L.M. Oberman. 2006. "Broken Mirrors: A Theory of Autism." *Scientific American* 295 (5): 62-9.

Schoenenwolf, Gerald. 1990. "Emotional Contagion: Behavioral Induction in Individuals and Groups." *Modern Psychoanalysis* 15 (1): 49-61.

Sheldrake, Rupert. 2009. *New Science of Life.* Icon Books.

van Kimmenade, Caroline. 2013. "Being Empathic versus Being an Empath: Crucial Differences." *The Happy Sensitive.* August 20. http://thehappysensitive.com/being-empathic-versus-being-empath-crucial-differences/.

Williamson, Marianne. 1996. *A Return to Love: Reflections on the Principles of "A Course in Miracles".* HarperOne.

World Health Organization. 11-14 October 1994. "Global Strategy on Occupational Health for All: The Way to Health at Work." *Second Meeting of the WHO Collaborating Centres in Occupational Health.* Beijing, China.

About the Authors

Aletheia Luna is an influential spiritual writer whose work has changed the lives of thousands of people worldwide. After escaping from the religious cult she was raised in, Luna experienced a profound existential crisis that led to her spiritual awakening. As an empath, mystic, and spiritual mentor, Luna's mission is to help others become conscious of their entrapment and find joy, empowerment, and liberation.

Mateo Sol is a prominent psychospiritual teacher whose work has influenced the lives of thousands of people worldwide. Born into a family with a history of drug addiction, abuse, and mental illness, Mateo Sol was taught about the plight of the human condition from a young age. As an empath, shaman, and spiritual guide, Sol's mission is to help others experience freedom, wholeness, and peace in any stage of life.

Together, Luna and Sol run the popular spiritual self-discovery website lonerwolf.com.

If you would like to discuss this book or talk with other empaths, you can join the Awakened Empath Group on **Facebook here:**
https://www.facebook.com/groups/AwakenedEmpath/

Other Books by the Authors

The Spiritual Awakening Process

Written for those who feel lost and alone in life, *The Spiritual Awakening Process* maps the journey of inner awakening and how to fulfill your personal destiny. With crystal clear and penetrating insight, spiritual mentors Luna and Sol help you to explore how to navigate through this chaotic life period in order to embody your highest calling. This book explores topics such as the dark night of the soul, soul loss, soul retrieval, inner child work, and many other topics which will help you to evolve into the awakened being you're destined to become.

Old Souls: The Sages and Mystics of Our World

Have you always felt older than what your age reflects? Are you solitary, thoughtful and intuitive? Do you feel like an outsider constantly looking into a society that doesn't feel like your home? If so, you may be an Old Soul. Existing as the perpetual outsiders in society, Old Souls are the teachers, counselors, philosophers and oracles of humanity. They are in the world, but are not quite of the world at the same time, passing through life on their own solitary paths. In this book, writer and researcher Aletheia Luna provides a compact, elegant and well-researched look into the life of Old Souls.